Woodrow Wilson:

an Anglophile war president
who fell in love with
England's
Lake District

John Coppack

To the memory of my half-sister
Joyce Coppack
who died in an air-raid on Liverpool
in 1941 aged two

ISBN 978-0-9562468-2-0

Front Cover: The head of Ullswater

Contents

Thomas Woodrow Wilson (1856-1924)

Introduction

Pelter Bridge, Rydal

This work owes its existence to a charming three-arched stone bridge providing a dry crossing of the River Rothay in England's Lake District. The centuries-old bridge stands in parkland at the foot of Loughrigg Fell close to the village of Rydal which lies between Ambleside and Grasmere. The poet William Wordsworth lived in Rydal from 1813 to his death in 1850. The Grade II listed bridge, known as Pelter Bridge, marks the start of one of the most popular circular fell walks in the region. I first came across the bridge in a work of fiction by Mrs Adelaide Victoria Arnold, an Edwardian writer of ghost stories, who featured the bridge in one of her novels.

In the course of carrying out research for a book I was writing on Mrs Arnold, I made a surprising discovery: Woodrow Wilson before he became the 28th president of the United States rented Loughrigg Cottage, which stands a little down stream from Pelter Bridge, where he and his first wife Ellen and their three daughters spent the summer of 1906. Writing to a friend upon arriving at his holiday home, Wilson

Introduction

remarked: "It is most picturesque and delightfully situated close by Rothay stream and under the shadow of Loughrigg, and though we are a tight fit, I am sure we shall be most comfortable and happy in it. It is at the heart of the region we most love."

My curiosity aroused I dug a little deeper and unearthed further revelations about the holiday habits of Woodrow Wilson before he became the 28th president of the United States. It turned out that Professor Wilson, who at the time was president of Princeton University, was a frequent visitor to the *Lake District. His first visit to the region was in the summer of 1896 when he cycled from Keswick to Windermere via Grasmere (in common with many Americans of his generation, Wilson had taken up the new craze of "wheeling"). His next visit was in the summer of 1899. On this occasion he was accompanied by his brother-in-law when the pair sought out places and shrines associated with Wilson's literary hero, William Wordsworth. His third visit was in the summer of 1903 when he came with his wife leaving behind their three daughters in the care of friends. During the course of their holiday they explored the northern lakes and cruised Ullswater on board a steam yacht. Wilson's fourth visit was when he rented Loughrigg Cottage above the banks of the River Rothay. During the course of his stay in 1906, Wilson was invited by Canon Rawnsley (one of the three founders of the National Trust) to witness the historic handing-over to the nation of Gowbarrow Park above the north-western shores of Ullswater. His fifth and final visit to Lakeland was in 1908 when he spent the summer in Grasmere with his Lake District friends. During the course of his holiday he explored on his bicycle the Duddon Valley and the far western lakes.

As the first decade of the new century was drawing to a close so too was Wilson's distinguished academic career. The transition from academia to the world of politics and public service was well underway leaving him with less time to indulge in long transatlantic voyages to Britain. Also by now the international situation was deteriorating. Britain and Germany were engaged in an arms race. Germany under the direction of Kaiser Wilhelm II and his Prussian commanders was rapidly

* Since 2017 a UNESCO World Heritage Site.

Introduction

building up her navy. Neither nation seemed capable of reversing the steady drift towards war.

When war finally erupted on European soil in the summer 1914, Woodrow Wilson was in his second term having occupied the White House since 1913 after winning the 1912 presidential election. Wilson was born in 1856 in the southern state of Virginia. His mother was born in the border town of Carlisle in north-west England. The family moved to North America in 1835. Wilson was the first United States president since Andrew Jackson to have had a parent born outside of America. His grandparents on his mother's side were born in Scotland and his grandparents on his father's side lived in County Tyrone, Ireland before emigrating to Ohio in 1807. Wilson grew up in a Presbyterian household and was a life-long member of the Presbyterian Church.

Wilson was a late developer and as a child exhibited the characteristics of dyslexia. Through dogged determination and self-discipline he overcame these early challenges to become one of the leading political scientists of his generation, head of a world-class university, the 28th president of the United States, the first president to hold a Ph.D degree, a Nobel peace laureate, a world statesman who was instrumental in founding the League of Nations (the forerunner of the United Nations) and the primary architect in reshaping the world following the defeat of the Central Powers in 1918.

Woodrow Wilson must be one of the most written-about politicians of the 20th-century. Every inch of his political and personal life has been dissected, analysed and evaluated on an industrial scale. No stone has been left unturned. Books, papers and articles expatiating his achievements and triumphs, his failures and mistakes, his idealism and morality, his distain of ostentation and pedantry, his obstinacy and arrogance, his two marriages and an extra-marital infatuation would fill a whole library. It is a brave – some would say foolish – writer who enters this congested field with a new book on this extraordinary man. But first a disclaimer. This work is not a cradle-to-grave biography. In fact it doesn't even qualify as a biography for it omits more about Wilson's life than it includes. The following chapters provide a snap-shot of Woodrow Wilson at certain phases of his life. Wilson's second term as president coincided with the Great War and the Paris Peace Conference. Both these seminal events had far reaching consequences that still haunt our world today.

Woodrow Wilson was undeniably an Anglophile. By inheritance he was from Scottish and Irish stock. His admiration for the British parliamentary system of government knew no limits; his heroes included Edmond Burke, Walter Bagehot and William Gladstone. Wilson loved English, Scottish and Irish literature especially the writings of 17th-and 18th-century authors such as Sir Thomas Browne, John Milton, Charles Lamb and above all Sir Walter Scott.

Woodrow Wilson was a profoundly emotional man, an incurable romantic, an idealist. Reading *The Farewell* by William Wordsworth would bring tears to his eyes. For many years he kept by his side *The Oxford Book of English Verse* which would accompany him on his foreign travels. Rudyard Kipling's famous motivational poem *IF* exhorting self-control, integrity and humility was a particular favourite, a copy of which he kept in his wallet. Wilson was a non-smoker and drank only moderately - Scotch whisky being his favourite tipple. When a young boy, he was taught not to take more food on his plate than he could eat, a habit that remained with him throughout his life. Wilson had a likening for the past and the old ways and customs. He loved visiting Britain's ancient cathedral towns. Ecclesiastical architecture had a special appeal. So did walled gardens, college quadrangles and centuries old dry stone walls characteristic of upland areas of Britain.

A combination of factors may have contributed to Wilson's Anglophilia. Being born in the South and a child of the Civil War may have left him with a residual, almost subconscious, antipathy towards the northern "Yankees". Southerners at the time had a tendency to idolize Great Britain. Although officially the United Kingdom remained neutral throughout the war supporting neither the Confederacy nor the North,

Introduction

in actuality it leaned towards the South notwithstanding slavery and segregation were antithetical to the former colonial power. The son of an English-born mother whose parents hailed from Scotland and Irish blood running through his veins will no doubt have played their part.

Nonetheless, lest it be thought that my subject was a surrogate Brit, Wilson was a devoted and passionate American patriot. He loved baseball, a game he played as a young man and throughout his life remained an ardent fan. He was an advocate of American football and encouraged the playing of the game amongst his students at Princeton. During his visit to London in the closing days of 1918, Woodrow Wilson poured cold-water on the idea that Americans are cousins of the British. Speaking to a senior British intelligence officer, Wilson cautioned against thinking of Americans "as cousins, still less as brothers. We are neither. Neither must you think of us as Anglo-Saxons, for that term can no longer be rightly applied to the peoples of the United States." One wonders what Wilson would have thought of the term "special relationship" coined by Winston Churchill at the end of the Second World War?

The following chapters are not presented in a chronological time-line. The book opens with Wilson's momentous address to Congress on April 2, 1917 when he called upon the lawmakers to declare war against Germany. The decision to enter the European conflict on the side of the Allies effectively sealed Germany's fate as an imperial power. For the first thirty-one months of the European War (as the Great War was known in America), the United States remained neutral although public opinion was generally pro-Britain and France.

The first chapter casts a spotlight on the events that moved the United States from a position of neutrality to full engagement in the war, a war, incidentally, in which two of my uncles (my father's brothers) fought on the Western Front. They both survived the terrible ordeal but their lungs were scared by "mustard gas" which ultimately cut short their lives. My father was too young to join his older brothers on the

Introduction

Western Front but he did play an active part in the Second World War as did my mother.

The second chapter focuses on the military situation prevailing on the Western Front prior to the United States entering the war. Neither Germany and its allies nor the combined forces of France and Britain and their allies could over-power the other during this stalemated phase of the war. The posting to France of General "Black Jack" Pershing and the steps taken by Woodrow Wilson to put his country on a war footing are highlighted alongside the fallout from Russia's capitulation following the October revolution in 1917. Germany's spring offensive in 1918, which almost brought about the collapse of the French army and placed the British forces on the back-foot as they were driven towards the Channel ports, is recalled. The second chapter concludes with the German spring assault strategically failing as Pershing with two million American soldiers under his command mounts a successful counter-offensive which, together with the contingents from France, Britain, Australia, Canada and the Dominions, over-power the German land army.

The third chapter provides a brief outline of Woodrow Wilson's early life and the challenges he faced as a child. The chapter includes a summary of his educational achievements, his brief flirtation with vocational law, his rise as a lecturer in politics and constitutional law, the books he wrote on the American constitution and its system of government, his election to the office of president of Princeton University and his successful program to extend the intellectual footprint of the university, and his two-year stint as Governor of New Jersey leading to the winning of the 1912 presidential election. The chapter concludes with a summary of President Wilson's first term legislative achievements which to this day form the main pillars underpinning the world's largest economy.

Chapter four is the most intrusive in this book for it provides an insight into Wilson's two marriages – the first to Ellen Louise Axson, the daughter of a Presbyterian minister, whose untimely death at the age of

Introduction

fifty-four led to a whirl-wind courtship and marriage to Edith Bolling Gault, a vivacious forty-two year old widow, seventeen years his junior, with a penchant for haute couture. Throughout his life Wilson had relatively few close male friends but he was susceptible to uncritical, adoring, intelligent women with a shapely figure. Edith, who worshipped the ground upon which he walked, was certainly one such woman. Another woman who entered into Wilson's life when his first marriage was going through difficulties was Mrs Mary Peck, a party-loving married woman who was estranged from her husband. The chapter touches upon Wilson's relationship with Mrs Peck – a relationship which down the years has been the subject of much speculation by his biographers, historians and even playwrights.

The fifth chapter headed "Lake District Summers" was a joy to write and photograph. For many years south Lakeland has been my second home. Wilson too loved this area especially "Wordsworth Country". As previously mentioned Professor Wilson first came to the Lake District in 1896 at a time when most people in Britain rarely travelled outside the county in which they were born. The fifteen day, 3000 nautical-mile, crossing of the Atlantic was made in primitive steamships often in storm-tossed seas with icebergs a lurking danger on the northern reaches of the passage. During his summer holidays in Britain, Wilson would have encountered many challenges not least the huge range of local dialects and accents. Wilson spoke American-English with a southern drawl and the locals he met en route – farmers and farmhands, shop and inn keepers, policemen and postmen, carriage drivers and others – may well have had difficulty in understanding him and he they. At the time tourism was nowhere as developed as it is today. The telephone had not reached rural locations, radio was still on the horizon and electricity was too expensive for most homes and businesses. The automobile had yet to establish itself. On the other hand Britain had an extensive rail network and its paved roads were the envy of Americans. One cannot but admire the spirit of this intrepid Princetonian professor travelling around Britain in the late Victorian era in search of his heroes.

Introduction

Chapter six fast-forwards to December 1918. The guns are silent but to formally end the Great War the combatant nations must first settle the terms of peace. Woodrow Wilson has emerged as the most powerful and authoritative statesman in the world. He decides, against advice, to attend in person the peace talks in Paris. But first he and the first lady have a number of ceremonial engagements to fulfill starting in France where they are received by the president and his wife. From France, the Wilsons head for London where they are met by King George V and Queen Mary. A state banquet hosted by the king and queen is held in their honour at Buckingham Palace. With the royal train placed at their disposal, the Wilsons travel overnight to Carlisle where the president is bestowed with the Freedom of the City. "A pilgrimage of the heart" is how Wilson described the visit to his mother's place of birth. With no time to visit the Lake District, the president and first lady depart for Manchester for yet another Freedom of the City honour (the fourth on his brief visit to England) and thence back to London.

Chapter Seven provides a brief account of the Paris Peace Conference which was formally opened on January, 18, 1919 and continued for six months. Over thirty nations participated in the talks but in reality it was the United States, Great Britain, France and Italy (known as the Big Four or, officially, the Council of Four) that set the agenda and made the major decisions. Wilson led the discussions and chaired the main meetings. His main goal was the formation of a League of Nations to settle territorial disputes before they erupted into full scale war. Britain, France and Italy had their own objectives – the League was not high on their agenda. The discussions were tortuous, glacially slow, frequently fractious with stand-offs and walk-outs. During the negotiations Wilson's health, never very robust at the best of times, deteriorated; he suffered from lapses of memory and was never fully on top of his brief. At times his temper got the better of him. David Lloyd George, who headed the British delegation, speculated that the president had suffered a stroke. By June the Big Four were in a position to present to the German Government the peace terms. Under duress representatives of the German Government signed the peace treaty in the great Palace of Versailles from which the treaty takes its name.

Introduction

Chapter Seven provides an overview of the main terms of the Versailles Treaty, a treaty which redrew the map of continental Europe and established nine new nation states. The treaty left many loose ends, the consequences of which are still being played out on the international stage to this day.

With the signing of the peace treaty, the presidential party left France for New York on June 29, 1919. The negotiations had taken a heavy physical and emotional toll on Wilson. The president's signature on the treaty establishing the League of Nations did not in and of itself legally bind the United States. Until Congress ratified the treaty the United States would remain outside its terms and still at war with Germany. The House of Representatives was broadly in favour of ratification but the Senate was sceptical with a whole body of Republican senators led by Wilson's formidable rival, Henry Cabot Lodge, hostile to ratification.

Chapter eight provides a brief account of the campaign mounted by Wilson to secure Congress's ratification of the treaty. Having failed to persuade the recalcitrant senators to support ratification, Wilson raises his standard by taking his case to the country and going over the heads of the senators. A one-month nationwide speaking tour by train is organised. Edith and her husband's physician have serious misgivings about such a long tour in blistering hot temperatures given the fragile state of Wilson's health. The president was not open to persuasion. The speaking tour went ahead but had to be aborted before it was completed due to the president's deteriorating health. The train driver was instructed to return to Washington DC post-haste. Within days of arriving back at the White House, the president suffered a near-fatal stroke leaving the left side of his body paralysed, his vision impaired and his mental state confused.

Chapter nine recalls the extraordinary steps taken by Edith Wilson and her husband's physician, acting as co-conspirators, to hide from members of Wilson's cabinet, members of Congress, the press and the American public the true extent of the president's illness and disability. From October 1919 to the end of Wilson's second term, the first lady managed the office of the president effectively assuming the role of

Introduction

de facto president. Some scholars and historians have regarded Edith Wilson as the first woman to occupy the office of president.

Woodrow Wilson never fully recovered from his stroke and the closing chapter provides an account of Wilson's life after leaving the White House up until his death three years later. During the dying days of his administration, Wilson planned what would have been his sixth visit to his beloved Lake District. Sadly, illness thwarted his holiday plans. But in the summer of 1925, his widow made her own "pilgrimage" to see for herself the beauties of Lakeland and the places her late husband loved so dearly.

J.C.
April 2023

PROLOGUE

"......that the action of the United States with its repercussions on the history of the world depended....upon the workings of this man's mind and spirit to the exclusion of almost every other factor....." Winston Churchill writing about Woodrow Wilson.

Spring had arrived and in the early morning sunlight the nation's capital was a kaleidoscope of colour. The sweet scent of apple and cherry blossom drifted through the air. The public squares and gardens were ablaze with the stunning blooms of magnolias and wisterias. The magnolia tree gracing the south lawn of the White House planted by Andrew Jackson in memory of his beloved wife was in full flight.

Shortly before eight o'clock on the morning of April 2, 1917 the chauffeur-driven presidential limousine drew up outside the White House. The 28th president of the United States Woodrow Wilson and his second wife Edith stepped inside the luxury automobile that was to take them to Chevy Chase, Maryland for a round of golf. Both the president and his wife were avid golfers although Edith was the more

The White House

PROLOGUE

accomplished player with a lower handicap. Wilson's lack of peripheral vision in his left eye affected his putting game. History does not record who won the round but Woodrow Wilson would frequently take up his clubs as an antidote to the pressure and stress of the presidency.

Wilson, a progressive Democrat, was in his second term having occupied the White House since 1913 after winning the 1912 presidential election. Over the weekend Wilson had confined himself to his private study on the second floor to work on the most important speech of his life. The speech drafted in his own hand and then written on his typewriter was now complete but its preparation had exacted a huge emotional toll on the author. A number of White House staff observed that during the drafting stage of the speech, Wilson was uncharacteristically "out of sorts" requesting solitude. Only the author, possibly Edith Wilson, and *Colonel Edward House, Wilson's confidential advisor, knew the contents of the speech. Even members of Wilson's cabinet had not been apprised in advance of its deliver which was to be given to a joint session of Congress later that day.

On returning to the White House from his early morning round of golf with the first lady, the president found himself at a loose end while he anxiously waited for Congress to call him to the chamber to deliver his address. Due to procedural wrangling between members of the two legislative chambers it was mid-afternoon before the call finally came to address members of Congress at eight-thirty that evening. For the second time that day the Wilsons boarded the presidential limousine that was to take them on the short journey to the Capitol. Wilson and Edith were accompanied by Margaret, the president's eldest daughter by his first marriage, and Helen Woodrow Bones, Wilson's first cousin and social secretary.

By now Washington was buzzing with rumours that the president was about to make a major speech to members of Congress concerning the worsening international situation. The ubiquitous streetcars crisscrossing the nation's capital were crammed with passengers, many

* Honorary title only. Edward House had no military service.

PROLOGUE

of whom were making their way to Capitol Hill where they would join thousands of like-minded citizens gathering at the western front of the Capitol.

The sun was setting over Georgetown as the presidential limousine with its escort of mounted cavalry and police outriders swept along Pennsylvania Avenue whose tree-lined side-walks were thronged with promenaders enjoying the warm spring evening. The president was a highly skilled and accomplished orator so it is unlikely he was racked by nerves as he sat in the plush automobile clutching his typewritten speech. But being a reflective and circumspect politician, the president may have had some reservations as to how his address would be received by Congress. Possibly, he was also contemplating the international repercussions his speech would have around the world.

At eight-thirty the president strode into the packed House Chamber to spontaneous applause from the House Representatives and Senators. Sensing that history was in the making many of the assembled members were enthusiastically waving small American flags. From their seats in the public gallery, Edith, Margaret and Helen watched the president ascend the marble rostrum where he placed his typed-written manuscript on the wooden lectern. With his hands resting on the lectern and without looking around the vast chamber the president in a sombre, restrained voice read from his manuscript.

"Gentlemen of the Congress

I have called Congress into extraordinary session because there are serious, very serious choices of policy to be made, and made immediately, which it was neither right nor constitutionally permissible that I should assume the responsibility of making."

Woodrow Wilson addressing a joint session of Congress on April 2, 1917. In his address Wilson asks Congress for a declaration of war against Germany. "The world must be made safe for democracy," became the defining message of his war address.

Chapter One

America First

"The plunge of civilization into this abyss of blood and darkness.....". Henry James writing to a friend the day after the United Kingdom entered the Great War.

Since the beginning of February the president had been confronted with a series of disturbing developments arising from the prosecution of the war in Europe by Germany, France, Russia, Great Britain and their allies. For a little over two-and-half years since the conflict first erupted in the summer of 1914, Wilson had skilfully, despite many provocations, steered the United States away from the maelstrom that was sucking in ever more nations into global warfare.

From the outset the president's approach to the war in Europe had been broadly aligned with public opinion in the United States. Whilst the public were mainly pro-Britain and France (pro-German sympathies were mainly confined to the people of German extraction who resided in New York, Chicago and the midwest states and amongst those members of the American-Irish community who supported Irish independence) the general consensus favoured the United States remaining neutral.

In August 1914, Wilson issued a statement to the press in which he cautioned the people of America not to become "divided in camps of hostile opinion, not against each other" notwithstanding their ties to nations at war. The United States "must be neutral in fact as well as in name during these times that are to try men's souls. We must be impartial in thought as well as in action, must put a curb upon our sentiments."

As the end of the year approached, Wilson admitted in a confidential interview with the *New York Times* that he did not believe Germany was solely to blame for the war, and that neither side ought to win a big victory. "I think that the chances of a just and lasting peace, and the only possible peace that will be lasting, will be happiest if no nation gets the decision by arms....."

America First

Predating Donald Trump, the 45th president of the United States, by ten decades, Woodrow Wilson adopted the slogan "America First" as part of his foreign policy. Wilson coined the phrase in a speech he gave to the annual luncheon of the Associated Press in New York on April 20, 1915:

So that I am not speaking in a selfish spirit when I say that our whole duty, for the present at any rate, is summoned up in this motto, "America First". Let us think of America before we think of Europe, in order that America may be fit to be Europe's friend when the day of tested friendship comes. The test of friendship is not now sympathy with one side or the other, but getting ready to help both sides when the struggle is over. The basis of neutrality, gentlemen, is not indifference, it is not self-interest. The basis of neutrality is sympathy for mankind. It is fairness, it is goodwill. At bottom it is impartiality of spirit and of judgment.

Sinking of the Lusitania London Illustrated News May 15, 1915

America First

The first major test of Wilson's proclaimed policy of neutrality came in February 1915 when Germany announced unrestricted warfare against all vessels flying neutral flags or otherwise that entered its declared war zone around the British Isles. In May 1915, the German embassy in Washington placed an advert in several New York newspapers reminding the public that Germany and Britain were at war and cautioned Americans intending to cross the Atlantic in British or allied ships did so at their own risk. On May 7, 1915, a German submarine spotted the British passenger ship *Lusitania* as she was steaming towards her home port of Liverpool six days after leaving her berth in New York. The commanding officer of the submarine, without warning, fired a torpedo into the starboard side of the *Lusitania*. The attack took place off the southern tip of Ireland and within the German declared war zone. The great liner, operated by Cunard, sank in eighteen minutes killing one thousand one hundred and ninety-five passengers of whom one hundred and twenty-eight were American. Seven hundred and sixty four passengers and crew survived the attack.

For Germany the sinking of the liner was a public relations disaster although the German Government sought to justify the torpedo attack on the grounds that the *Lusitania* was carrying weapons, thus making it a legitimate target. Public opinion in America was incensed. Anti-German sentiment hardened as the full scale of the atrocity became apparent. Former President Roosevelt called for immediate action by the United States Government, referring to the sinking as "warfare against innocent women and children". Senior politicians on both sides of the aisle implored the president to take action. For Woodrow Wilson the sinking was a diplomatic nightmare, placing an enormous strain on relations between Washington and Berlin.

Wilson had pacifist tendencies but he was not a full-blooded pacifist. Despite his Anglophile leanings he was desperate to maintain America's neutrality in the war. However, he could not allow the U-boat torpedo attack on the *Lusitania* and the sinking of other vessels by German submarines to go unchecked. On July 21, 1916, Wilson issued an ultimatum to the German Government to the effect that the United

States would regard any subsequent sinking as "deliberately" unfriendly", the implication being that if Germany continued its policy of unrestricted submarine warfare the United States would take whatever action it deemed necessary to protect its interests. Wilson chose his words carefully for he did not want to box himself into a corner by threatening all out war in the event of further attacks.

Wilson's ultimatum had the desired effect. Kaiser Wilhelm II overruled his naval commanders and ordered that action against ships flying neutral flags be suspended. However, the suspension was short-lived. From the outset of the war, the British and French mounted a naval blockade of Germany. The Royal Navy, the largest and most powerful navy in the world at the time, played the dominant role in policing the blockade, the purpose of which was to restrict the supply of goods and raw materials from fuelling the German war machine.

The British and French naval blockade was having a devastating effect upon the German economy. Shortages of raw materials, food, clothes and essential supplies impeded the prosecution of the war. More significantly the embargo was leading to severe food shortages. Malnutrition was endemic. Looting and food riots were breaking out across Germany. Morale amongst the German people was at a low ebb; the public were becoming increasingly disillusioned with the war, a war which many thought would be over in days and certainly by Christmas 1914.

By now Germany was under the virtual military dictatorship of two supreme army commanders, Erich von Ludendorff and Paul von Hindenburg both Prussians who between them not only directed the war effort but ruled Germany without regard for Germany's (wafer-thin) constitution. With the ascendancy of the duumvirate, Kaiser Wilhelm II had become a marginalised figure in state affairs although he still retained the affection of his subjects.

With the German economy close to collapse, Ludendorff and Hendenberg were desperate for a breakthrough in the war and persuaded an increasing erratic and insecure kaiser to order the resumption from February 1, 1917 of unrestricted submarine warfare. In signing the order, the German emperor acknowledged that unleashing his submarines once again would lead to the United States entering the war on the side of the Allies.

On January 31, 1917, the German ambassador in Washington paid a visit to the State Department to announce that from midnight his nation would begin unrestricted submarine warfare. According to Colonel Edward House, "The president was sad and depressed" and whilst refusing to believe that war was inevitable he suspended diplomatic relations with Germany.

The resumption of unrestricted submarine warfare (the German High Command was careful not to provoke America by attacking vessels flying the stars and stripes) did not materially change American public opinion which was still broadly in favour of remaining on the sidelines of the conflict.

During the 1916 presidential election both Wilson and his Republican opponent Charles Evan Hughes, a former Supreme Court justice, ran on an "America First" platform. In appealing to those voters who wanted no truck with the war in Europe, Wilson's campaign team deployed the popular slogan "He kept us out of war."

Wilson by a smaller margin than four years earlier (the Republican party, unlike the 1912 election, fielded a unified candidate in Hughes) won both the popular vote and secured a narrow majority in the Electoral College. Wilson was the first Democrat since Andrew Jackson in 1832 to win two consecutive terms.

On February 24, 1917, the contents of a sensational telegram (which had been decoded by British naval intelligence) were relayed to Woodrow Wilson. The author of the telegram was Arthur Zimmermann, the German foreign secretary. The coded telegram was wired to his country's ambassador in Mexico city instructing the ambassador to make contact with the president of Mexico offering a military alliance should the United States declare war on Germany following Germany's decision to recommence unrestricted submarine warfare.

The contents of the telegram were published in the American press one week after disclosure to Wilson. "U.S. BARES WAR PLOT" ran the headline in the *Chicago Tribune* on March 1, 1917. Unsurprisingly, public opinion was enraged. The proposed military alliance between Germany and Mexico was akin to waving a red rag in front of an American bull. However, it was the second part of the telegram that was nothing short of incendiary – in exchange for "generous financial support and an understanding on our part that Mexico is to recover the lost territory in Texas, New Mexico and Arizona" ceded to the United States in the aftermath of the Mexican-American War close to seventy years earlier.

The *Zimmermann Telegram,* coupled with Germany's resumption of unrestricted submarine activity leading to the sinking of four United States merchant ships with fifteen American seafarers losing their lives, stirred up anti-German sentiment and tipped the scales of public opinion from one of neutrality to engagement in the conflict.

As unwelcome as it was, the *Zimmermann Telegram* did not, per se, force Wilson to change direction. He still sought to avoid war, if at all possible, despite recent provocations by the Germans. But for the first time since the conflict had erupted in the summer of 1914, Wilson was no longer in lock-step with public opinion which was now baying – egged on by a jingoistic press – for military involvement in the war.

However, by the time Wilson gave his second inaugural address on Monday, March 5, 1917 (an address in which he once again proclaimed his aversion to war) he had in fact moved a step closer to putting the country on a war footing.

America First

Just days before his inaugural address, Wilson had asked Congress (which following the election was still controlled by Democrats) for authority to place guns on American merchant vessels. The lower house passed the bill but it was timed-out when it came before the upper house. A small group of dissident senators determined to maintain America's neutrality banded together in making lengthy speeches opposing the bill. One senator said that the United States had entered "a twilight zone between war and peace". Not for the first time, nor indeed the last, a bad-tempered and disgruntled president decided to bypass Congress by issuing an executive order – henceforth American ships crossing the Atlantic would be armed with guns manned by naval personnel. By adopting a position of "armed neutrality" as he called it, Wilson was anticipating trouble in the coming days and weeks.

March was turning into Wilson's own *mensis horribilis* The worsening international situation was causing the president considerable distress. He looked "haggard and worried" wrote one journalist. According to Frank Cobb, the Editor of the *New York World*, who met the president on March 19, he was "lying awake at night going over the whole situation". During this difficult period the president isolated himself in the White House receiving few callers and declined speaking engagements. He rarely left 1600 Pennsylvania Avenue other than to play golf – a sure sign that he was under considerable stress.

In mid-March the gloom was lifted momentarily when news reached the White House that Nicholas II of Russia had abdicated following civil unrest in Petrograd (formerly St Petersburg). The war was going badly for Russia. Its armies were being annihilated by the combined forces of Germany and Austro-Hungary. The Russian people had lost faith in the corrupt tsarist regime. Scarcity of food had brought them out onto the streets of the capital. Troops were deployed to quell the riots but many defected to the side of the protestors. On March 15, Nicholas II abdicated the throne in favour of his brother Michael who refused the crown, thus bringing to an end three hundred years of rule by the Romanov dynasty. A new Provincial Government was formed to restore order and prosecute the war more effectively. But by now the poorly equipped and trained Russian troops had lost the will to fight.

America First

The Russian losses were staggering – well in excess of one million dead plus untold casualties. Britain and France implored the new Provincial Government to continue the war effort in order to relieve the pressure their own land armies were under on the Western Front but the Russian forces were too broken and demoralised. Although it was a double-edged sword, Wilson welcomed the news of the tsar's abdication. The United States was the first foreign government to recognise the new Provincial Government in Petrograd.

The domestic economic situation bought about by the war was rising rapidly up the White House agenda. By March 1917, the United States and the allied nations had become inextricably entwined economically. Both blocks had become co-dependent on each other. When war broke out in Europe, America was in a deep recession, the stock market had fallen off a cliff and unemployment was on a steep upward trajectory. As the war intensified and orders for munitions, raw materials and foodstuffs came flooding in from the Allies, the economic situation was transformed. Idle factories and shipyards were now working flat-out to provide the Allies with goods, ships and materials to fight and sustain the war. American farmers, especially growers of wheat, were enjoying boom conditions on the back of orders placed by the Allies. The enormous financial aid America was now providing to the allied nations in the form of loans (loans that had to be repaid after the war) placed the United States more firmly in the Allies' camp. As the war entered its third year, the allied nations had exhausted their lines of credit. Britain, France, Italy and Russia now looked to Wall Street to bank-roll the purchase of foodstuffs, munitions and other essential supplies necessary to sustain the war effort. The British economist John Maynard Keynes held that the Allied war effort was becoming totally dependent on supplies and credit from America. Wall Street was broadly sympathetic to the plight of Britain and France and had bet the farm on the Allies defeating the Central Powers.

The industrial scale carnage taking place in Europe was overshadowing all discourse on whether the United States should change its policy on neutrality and self-imposed isolationism by declaring war on Germany. When the kaiser's army marched into neutral Belgium in the summer of 1914, the German High Command did not foresee that the campaign to defeat the French army by bypassing the defensive fortifications built by France along its border with Germany would get bogged-down in trench warfare along a 400-mile corridor of land running from the North Sea through Belgium and France down to the Swiss border. Neither the Imperial German army nor the joint British and French forces were able to defeat the other in great set battles as both opponents tried in vain to out flank the other ostensibly to gain a small territorial advantage that would be lost when the next big push came from the other side. Many combatant nations have found to their cost that starting a war rarely goes according to plan and all too frequently ends in protracted bloody catastrophes. Russia's unlawful invasion of Ukraine in February 2022 underscores the point.

When Britain sent an expeditionary force to oppose the German advance into Belgium, its military commanders schooled in 19th-century colonial warfare techniques were taken aback by the scale and intensity of the German war machine. As Britain's losses mounted regular troops were supplemented by territorials and a whole army of volunteers drawn from all corners of the British Isles. Courageous as the volunteers undoubtedly were they were no match when pitted against a professional army deploying a battery of heavy artillery fire, machine guns, flame-throwers, toxic gas shells and a band of defensive barbed wire. On one day alone above the banks of the River Somme in northern France nearly twenty thousand British soldiers lost their lives in a sea of mud and blood trying to push back the German defensive positions.

American journalists, who had greater access to the European fronts than their European counterparts and were not working under strict censorship regulations, were regularly reporting back to their newspapers on the massed battles taking place between the combatants and the grievous blood drain. Such reports along with intelligence information Wilson was receiving from his ambassadors in London, Berlin and Paris served to inform him of the likely consequences in both human terms and the financial cost of entering into the war.

America First

Wilson knew that in order to secure victory over Imperial Germany, the United States would have to mobilise the nation and commit hundreds of thousands of young soldiers, sailors and airmen to the armed struggle, many of whom would never return to their homeland alive. Of those fortunate to survive the terrible ordeal, thousands would return home broken in mind and body, many would never work again.

And then there was the financial cost of putting the nation on a full-scale war footing – training and equipping soldiers, navy and air-crews, transporting troops across the Atlantic, mobilizing industry for the manufacture of ships, tanks, artilleries, aeroplanes, jeeps, munitions and all the paraphernalia required to equip a 20th-century army to fight a mechanised war overseas – and all to be paid for by increasing taxes and raising loans.

Faced with such a concatenation of events it is unsurprising that Wilson was unable to sleep at night as his mind worked over-time on trying to square the circle. No president since Abraham Lincoln had been called upon to decide the fate of the nation. To intervene in the war would not only change the direction of the war itself but it would also change the nature and ethos of American society for it would effectively propel a sleeping industrial giant with a population of a one hundred and twenty million out of the shadows where it had languished since the end of the Civil War onto the world-stage. It would only be a matter of time before America would take up the mantle of an exhausted United Kingdom.

By entering into the war, the United States would be jettisoning a convention beginning with George Washington of not getting involved in foreign entanglements. Thomas Jefferson in his inaugural address summed up America's doctrine of isolationism with the words "peace, commerce, and honest friendship with all nations, entangling alliances with none....." This doctrine applied, *a fortiori*, to Europe given that the United States was peopled largely drawn from the nations of Europe. By entering into the European war this long-established precedent of neutrality and isolationism, at least in terms of *Europe, would be confined to history.

Despite all his misgivings, natural caution and profound aversion to war, Wilson eventually came round to the view that America's best interests would be served by entering into the conflict on the side of Britain and France. America's active involvement in the war, reasoned Wilson, would tip the military balance decidedly in favour of the Allies, thus shortening a stalemated war where neither side could muster enough assets in manpower and equipment to over-power the other, although the German army at times came close to breaking through the defensive lines of the Anglo-French forces. Moreover – and this was probably the clincher for Wilson – the United States would in his calculation emerge from the war as the supreme world power, economically and militarily, thus placing the nation in a commanding position to impose a peace settlement on terms that would not only end the present world war with its ever mounting casualties but all future wars – a war to end all wars.

At a crucial cabinet meeting held on March 20, its members unanimously supported war. The following day Wilson issued a call for Congress to meet on April 2. Under the United States constitution only Congress can declare war and as commander-in-chief of the armed forces it falls upon the president to ask Congress to declare war.

*Outside the European arena the United States went to war with Mexico in 1846 and with Spain (fought in the Caribbean and Pacific) in 1898 over Cuba, Puerto Rico and the Philippine islands.

Chapter Two

War

"The world must be made safe for democracy." Woodrow Wilson addressing a joint session of Congress on April 2, 1917.

Wilson began his war address to Congress by reviewing Germany's maritime transgressions – the use by Germany of its submarines which he described as "cruel and unmanly" resulting in vessels being "ruthlessly sent to the bottom" and the German Government's "reckless lack of compassion". Wilson reminded the legislators that "unrestricted" deployment of submarines is a violation of international law and a "warfare against mankind". He cited the *Zimmerman Telegram* as evidence of Germany's "hostile purpose". Wilson admitted that his policy of "armed neutrality" is "impracticable".

Following his review of the maritime situation, the president then called on Congress to declare war against Germany but importantly he drew a distinction between the autocratic Imperial German Government and the German people. "We have no quarrel with the German people." Wilson then broadened this principle by informing Congress that we are going to fight "for the ultimate peace of the world and the liberation of its peoples, the German people included". "The world must be made safe for democracy." This sentence became the defining message of Wilson's war address, the raison d'etre for his calling for a declaration of war against Germany.

(It is doubtful whether Wilson realized that in writing and then uttering "The world must be made safe for democracy" he was laying down the cornerstone upon which American foreign policy in the Second World War, NATO, Vietnam, the Middle East and alliances with Japan and South Korea would be built. More recently, America's role as the "world's policeman" has been questioned by influential American politicians. Donald Trump in his early pronouncements appeared to lean towards the doctrine of isolationism as advocated by George Washington and Thomas Jefferson.)

War

In his speech the president looked beyond the existing conflict to a new world order and the creation of an international body that would maintain world peace "....a steadfast concert for peace can never be maintained except by a partnership of democratic states", declared Wilson. Here the President was setting down the principle of an International League of Peace which in 1920 took the form of the League of Nations, the precursor of the United Nations.

Wilson concluded his thirty minute war address by reiterating that German policy had forced us into war "because there are no other means of defending our rights". His concluding passage amounted to an emotional appeal to the Almighty. Paraphrasing Martin Luther's declaration, he ends his war address with the words: "God helping me, I can do no other."

These divine words were followed by a momentary silence before the House Chamber erupted into wild cheering and flag waving. *Congressmen and senators fell over each other to congratulate the president on his momentous address. Henry Cabot Lodge, a distinguished Republican senator, took Wilson by the hand and said: "Mr Wilson you have expressed in the loftiest manner possible the sentiments of the American people." The masses who had assembled outside the Capitol joined in the chorus of ecstatic cheering although it is unlikely in those pre-radio and television days the crowds actually heard the speech, just the resounding cheering echoing around the House Chamber at its conclusion.

Wilson had delivered the most important speech of his life – a speech not of towering oratory but a solemn address carefully crafted to persuade members of Congress that in calling for a declaration of war against Germany, the United States stood firmly on the moral high ground and if the world was to be made safe for democracy there was no alternative but to fight "for the rights and liberties of small nations".

Following the recommendation of the president, Congress – after much heated debate – passed the War Resolution with three hundred and

*Apologies to Jeannette Rankin of Montana, the first woman elected to Congress in 1916.

seventy-three votes in favour and fifty votes against. In the Senate the margin was eighty-two in favour of war and six against. On April, 5, 1917, the War Resolution was presented to the president who signed his approval using his wife's fountain pen.

Wilson never wanted to be a war president. In the words of Colonel Edward House, he was "not well fitted" to be a war president, "he was too refined, too civilized, too intellectual, too cultivated not to see the incongruity and absurdity of war". Nonetheless, during the next eighteen months Wilson proved to be a highly effective war president. It is beyond the scope of this work to detail the careful planning that went into the economic and military mobilization of the United States. Suffice to say that Wilson, recognising his limitations across a range of subjects, delegated the economic mobilization to men such as Herbert Hoover, the financier Bernard Baruch and his son-in-law, William Gibbs McAdoo.

On military matters, especially the raising of an expeditionary force to fight in Europe, Wilson delegated the task to professional soldiers. Perhaps the most important appointment made by Wilson was that of General "Black Jack" Pershing to command what would become the American Expeditionary Force in Europe. Wilson gave the recently widowed Pershing carte blanche to conduct military operations as he thought fit. In fact Wilson and Pershing only met once during the entire time the United States was engaged in the war. Unlike many world leaders who cannot resist the urge to micro-manage military operations, Wilson was quite content to leave operational matters to those whose expertise was greater than his.

General Pershing and his staff landed in France in June 1917. Their first task was to prepare an organizational plan that called for an army of one million men by 1918 and three million by 1919. From a standing army of only one hundred and twenty-seven thousand officers and soldiers, the mobilization, training and transportation of so many troops required meticulous planning and a high-level of organizational skills which under the team assembled by Wilson more than met the challenge.

War

"Over there, over there....Send the word, send the word over there.....
That the Yanks are coming....The Yanks are coming....The drums rum
tumming Ev'rywhere....." George M Cohan (1917).

Following the declaration of war, the Broadway entertainer George M Cohan penned the patriotic song *Over There* which included the famous chorus line "The Yanks are coming". The Yanks were indeed on their way to the Western Front but at first their numbers were a mere trickle. It was not until October 1917 that the First Division entered the trenches at Nancy in France. The slow build up of combat ready troops reflected Pershing's desire to have an American force that could operate independently of Britain and France.

At the beginning of the European war, the United States possessed a powerful regional navy but in world terms it was not one of the major fleets. Under the overall direction of Wilson, the United States' fleet grew by a factor of eight and ended the war a naval super-power. Supported by the Royal Navy and assisted by the United States Coast Guard, the most significant contribution the United States navy made during the war was the escort and transport across to France of two million *doughboys.

Another significant contribution made by the United States navy was in persuading a reluctant Admiralty (a British Government department responsible for maritime affairs) to adopt the convoy system for protecting merchant shipping (as opposed to troop transits). At the time Wilson called on Congress to declare war against Germany, one in four ships bound for Britain were being sunk by German U-boats. This toll on merchant shipping was not only impeding Britain's ability to effectively prosecute the war, it was reducing the importation of staple foodstuffs. At the height of the submarine campaign Britain had a mere six weeks' food supply which was being eked-out by rationing. The convoy strategy proved to be highly effective in overcoming and eventually defeating the German submarine campaign aimed at starving the people of Britain into submission.

* The popular nickname of American soldiers The etymology is uncertain but thought to have first appeared in the Mexican-American War of 1846-1848.

Spring in the Trenches, Ridge Wood 1917 by Paul Nash.
Credit: Imperial War Museum

War

The arrival in France of American service men – at first in penny numbers but eventually in hundreds of thousands – rejuvenated a flagging war campaign that France and Britain and their allies were struggling to mount against a superior German land army. During the first half of the war, the British army, notwithstanding the bravery of individual soldiers, performed poorly when measured against a more professional, armed to the teeth and better led German force. Military historians will argue over the reasons for the disparity between the two forces. Indifferent command and control, small peace-time army augmented by a huge influx of poorly trained and equipped volunteers, a ridged class-based personnel system and, above all, a deficiency of armaments are often cited as reasons why the British army performed poorly on the battlefield. By 1917 many of these shortcomings were in the process of being rectified. The appointment of the energetic Welshman David Lloyd George as minister of munitions and eventually in December 1916 replacing the ineffectual Herbert Henry Asquith as head of the Liberal Government added urgency and dynamism to the war that had by now become one of attrition.

By the spring of 1917, both Britain and France were militarily – and financially – exhausted. Following big setbacks on the battlefields, morale amongst the French troops was at a low ebb. Mutinies were breaking out with men refusing to carry out orders of their commanders. Whilst the mutineers were willing to defend their positions in the trenches, they refused to go "over the top" on suicidal missions. Discipline amongst the British troops was better despite the horrendous slaughter taking place and general lack of progress. By now Italy had joined the Allies but its army was no match for the Austrians who roundly defeated the Italian contingent at Caporetto.

As 1917 wore on the situation of the Allies – desperate as it was – was about to become infinitely far worse. The crumbling of the Eastern Front following the overthrow of the Russian tsar enabled the Germans to transfer redundant divisions to the Western Front, thus placing the Allies under further strain. The deployment of the tank by the Anglo-French armies (which in the final year of the war helped turn the tide in favour of the Allies) was of limited value. The early designs were great lumbering giants, difficult to operate and prone to mechanical failure especially climbing in and out of deep shell craters.

The new year brought no respite from the dire situation facing Britain and France. The second Russian revolution in October 1917 brought the Bolshevik party led by Vladimir Lenin to power plunging the country into civil war. The new Communist government under the leadership of Lenin unilaterally ceased hostilities against the Central Powers. An armistice was signed on December 15, 1917 at Brest-Litovsk (a city in what today is Belarus close to the Polish border). This effectively took Russia, Belarus and Ukraine out of the war.

With Russia, Belarus and Ukraine no longer engaged in the conflict, the Germans were in a position to transfer the bulk of their forces from the eastern sector to the Western Front which for the first time gave them a numerical advantage over the Anglo-French armies. The British Government with Lloyd George at the helm was reluctant to replace "the fallen" with further conscripts. The influx of new blood from the east reinvigorated the German campaign. In the spring of 1918, Erich von Ludendorff's "stormtroopers" in a final throw of the dice launched an almighty onslaught against the British and French positions.

General Ludendorff's objective was to defeat the armies of Britain and France in one final big push by first driving a wedge between the British and French forces and then to overwhelm the British army before the Americans could ship sufficient *doughboys* across the Atlantic to turn back the tide. Ludendorff almost succeeded. In fact tactically he succeeded brilliantly. His offensive yielded large tracts of territory, capturing ninety thousand enemy soldiers in the process. His "stormtroopers" ("the flower of the German army" in the words of Lloyd George) came within shelling distance of Paris, and pushed the British forces towards the English Channel in a pre-run of 1940. One British soldier wrote that he "could taste the tang of the sea". Operationally, however, the German offensive failed.

War

In mounting its spring offensive, the Germany army sustained heavy losses particularly amongst its elite troops which could not be replaced in time for the next big battle. Ludendorff had imposed no limitation on the German advance resulting in over-stretched supply lines. Consequently the advancing German troops were left stranded, largely bereft of food and ammunition, and highly vulnerable to counter-attacks. Strategically, Ludendorff's big gamble had failed. The momentum was now with the Allies and the United States. By August 1918, the Americans had in France one million troops with ten thousand poring in every day. After four years of trench warfare the Anglo-French forces were by now pretty battle-hardened. Improved design of tanks were now being deployed in greater numbers along with aircraft. For the first time in the war the French and British armies had a unified command and control structure headed by General Ferdinand Foch. Full-frontal attacks resulting in huge casualties were no longer the order of the day.

Canadians going "over the top" to retake the French village of Neuville-Vitasse from the Germans in August 1918. Credit: Canadian War Museum.

War

In July 1918, General Foch began the counter-offensive beginning with the Battle of Amiens which delivered a decisive blow against an increasingly fatigued and demoralized enemy. During the next one hundred days the French, British and American armies supported by Canadian and Australian contingents launched a series of powerful counter-offensives against the German defensive positions.

WALKING WOUNDED

By August General Pershing had enough troops to mount independent full-frontal offences at St Mihiel and in the Meuse-Argonne. The Battle of Meuse-Argonne, the largest in United States military history, involved over a million *doughboys* of whom twenty-six thousand lost their lives. The battle signalled the end of the war. The main German army had retreated to the heavily fortified Hindenburg Line.

After four years of fighting and untold deaths and casualties, the Germans found themselves back where they where in September 1914.

Following heavy bombardment by British artillery on September 29, the Hindenburg Line was finally breached. German troops were now in full-flight, broken in spirit, completely demoralised. The situation was spiralling out of control and with no hope of retrieving the military situation, Hindenburg and Ludendorff advised the German Government that the war was lost and to seek an immediate armistice if total catastrophe was to be avoided.

War

Inside Germany events were also rapidly spiralling downhill. Civil unrest had broken out amongst the starving population. A whiff of revolutionary fervour was in the air. In early October, the German Government, behind the backs of the British and French, approached Woodrow Wilson (who was receiving regular reports about the fighting) with an offer to negotiate an armistice. Not surprisingly, the response from Wilson was unfavourable.

On October 26, Kaiser Wilhelm II finally summoned up the courage to dismiss an increasingly unhinged Ludendorff. Three days later the kaiser left Berlin for the military headquarters at Spa in Belgium. He never returned to the German Fatherland. On November 9, 1918, Kaiser Wilhelm II abdicated after Woodrow Wilson made it clear to the German Government that there could be no peace while Germany was under a virtual military dictatorship. The following day the kaiser boarded the royal train bound for the Netherlands where he spent the remainder of his life in exile. The former German Emperor died in 1941.

On November 7, Paul von Hindenburg contacted General Ferdinand Foch with a request to negotiate an armistice. On the morning of November 8 a delegation headed by the German secretary of state Matthias Erzberger met the Allied Supreme Commander in his railway carriage at a siding in the Forest of Compiègne in northern France. A final meeting between Erzberger and Foch and their respective teams took place in the early hours of November 11. Erzberger was presented with a set of non-negotiable terms to end the war. Just before sunrise, Erzberger on the instructions of Hindenburg signed the armistice. And at eleven o'clock on the morning of November 11, 1918 the guns across the Western Front fell silent. It is estimated that between fifteen and twenty-four million people, military and civilian, died in the conflict making it one of the worst in history.

War

"The American Army through its numbers, through its bravery of its troops and the skill of its leaders, is likely to prove the decisive factor in this War." Herbert Samuel addressing the British House of Commons on August 7, 1918.

The contribution made by the United States was recognised in a speech made by the British statesman Herbert Samuel in the House of Commons on August 7, 1918.

The House will, I am sure, join with the prime minister in his expression of profound admiration for the really wonderful achievement of the American Government and people in sending over in so brief a space a million and a third men across the Atlantic, in spite of difficulties of shipping, in spite of the perils of the submarine. It was the most marvellous achievement in transportation. I suppose no such large proportion of the human family has ever been transported by water in so short a space since the Flood. The American Army through its numbers, through the bravery of its troops, and the skill of its leaders, is likely to prove the decisive factor in this War.

Zonnebeke (1918) Sir William Orpen. Credit: Tate, London.

*War Memorial at Beaune, France honouring the fallen. France lost one
million, three hundred thousand military personnel in the Great War, a far
higher proportion of its pre-war population than any other combatant
nation.*

Chapter Three

Manse to the White House

Thomas Woodrow Wilson was born in the small rural town of Staunton, Virginia on December 28, 1856. He was the third child and first son of Joseph Ruggles Wilson and Janet Wilson. His father was a Presbyterian minister who had relocated from Ohio. Wilson's mother, Janet, was born in Carlisle in the county of Cumberland on December 26, 1826. (Wilson was the first United States president since Andrew Jackson to have a parent born outside of America.) Her father, Reverend Thomas Woodrow (originally spelt *Wodrow*), was born in Scotland (as was her mother, Marion Woodrow née Williamson) and relocated to Carlisle as minister of the local Congregational Church where he preached from 1820 to 1835, the year he moved the family to Brockville in Canada and eventually settling in Ohio, first in Chillicothe and later in Columbus.

In later life Woodrow Wilson would regale with amusement how close he became to not being born. During a stormy passage across the Atlantic, his mother was nearly swept overboard. Wilson's grandmother, Marion Woodrow, became very ill during the crossing and died shortly afterwards. Wilson's grandparents on his father's side lived in County Tyrone in Ireland (now one of the six counties that make up Northern Ireland) before emigrating to Steubenville, Ohio in 1807.

Woodrow Wilson's mother married Joseph Ruggles Wilson, the son of Judge Wilson, on June 7, 1849. According to sources Joseph had married well for the Woodrows had a higher social standing than the Wilsons. Joseph was tall, handsome and quite a hit amongst his female parishioners. The future president of the United States would have been the first to admit that the good-looks of his father had not been passed down to his first born son. Photographs, portraits and film-footage of Woodrow Wilson reveal an angular face with a strong, thrusting jaw that made him instantly recognisable. Later in life his prominent jaw would be a gift to cartoonists. He seems to have inherited from his mother a high forehead and blue-grey eyes. Her young son had a longish nose and prominent ears. In adult life Wilson had according to more than one source "astonishingly bad teeth". One unkind political opponent likened him to "an apothecary's clerk". But as a young man and later in life Wilson was not entirely unattractive being of moderate build and standing an inch below six foot which for someone born in the mid-19th-century was above average height.

During his childhood and adolescence Tommy Wilson (the name by which he was known before he dropped "Tommy" in favour of "Woodrow" which he considered to be more refined) enjoyed reasonably good health. However, from early adulthood his health deteriorated – the rest of his life was marred by recurring bouts of ill health. He had poor eyesight and from the age of eight wore glasses and at twenty-nine a retinal haemorrhage left him with poor vision in his left eye. Towards the end of his life he was almost blind.

Tommy Wilson was a late developer – nine before he could read. Even in later life he was a slow reader. More than one biographer has suggested that Wilson in his reading and writing exhibited the characteristics of dyslexia although unlike many dyslexics he was exceptionally good at spelling and grammar. Whether the young Tommy was dyslexic or whether it was his poor eyesight that impaired his reading is arguable. But what is not in doubt, Wilson through dogged determination and self-discipline overcame these challenges to become one of the leading political scientists of his generation, head of a world-class university, the 28th president of the United States, the first president to hold a Ph.D degree, a Nobel peace laureate, a world statesman who was instrumental in founding the League of Nations (the forerunner of the United Nations) and the main architect in reshaping the world after the demise of four empires – German, Russian, Austro-Hungarian and Ottoman – in the wake of the First World War.

Wilson's childhood was influenced and informed by the Presbyterian Church (of which he became a life-long member) and the American Civil War (1861-1865). Wilson, now living in Georgia, was only four years of age when war between the Confederacy and the Union erupted and eight when it ended. Wilson's parents were ardent supporters of the Confederacy led by Jefferson Davis. The most divisive political issue in America during the 19th-century was that of black slavery. The Confederacy – comprising eleven southern states including Georgia – wanted to maintain segregation between white and black people and, most controversially, maintain slavery. After four years of bitter fighting, the Union led by Abraham Lincoln won the Civil War. Slavery was abolished across the United States in 1865.

It is beyond the remit of this work to examine how being brought up in a southern slavery state, the Civil War and post-war reconstruction informed and shaped Wilson's attitudes and views on slavery, black emancipation and segregation. Wilson grew up in neighbourhoods populated by black people. His parents engaged more than one black servant although they were not slaves. As a young man Wilson once proclaimed: "I have very little ease with coloured people and they with me. Why is it? For I care enormously about them." It would seem from an early age Wilson had a problematic relationship with black people.

Based on the works of his biographers and scholars who have studiously examined Wilson's life, his endorsement of the policy of segregation in federal departments upon becoming president, the diary of the daughter of a close artist friend in which he is over-heard making racist remarks and other sources, it is difficult not to conclude that Woodrow Wilson was a racist as that term is understood today but his racism fell short of being a "white supremacist". Throughout his political life, Wilson was dismissive of actions designed to promote the advancement of black Americans. His segregationist ideology has been deplored by both the white and black communities and represents an irremovable stain on his legacy.

Despite his reading difficulties, Tommy Wilson was determined to pursue an academic career. After early schooling, Wilson enrolled with Davidson College in North Carolina and after a year transferred to the College of New Jersey (now Princeton University) where he excelled intellectually and academically. By now he had dropped the name

"Tommy" in favour of "Woodrow". While still an undergraduate, Wilson published a paper on the merits of the British parliamentary system. He was very much influenced by the writings of the 18th-century Irish-born British statesman, Edmund Burke. So swayed by the writings of Burke that Wilson told a confidant: "If I should claim any man as my master that man would be Burke."

Later on Wilson was to develop further his interest in the British constitution by writing a book comparing the American Government with the British parliamentary and cabinet model. His penchant for the British parliamentary system of government (with the prime minister at its head with ultimate responsibility for the legislative program) over the United States Constitution (with the president vested with executive powers but not legislative ones other than the power of veto) possibly derived from an affinity with his Scottish-Irish heritage and pride in his English-born mother.

A pensive young graduate

After graduation in 1879, Wilson embarked on a course of legal studies at the University of Virginia Law School in the hope that a qualification in law would lead into politics, a subject close to his heart. Poor health forced Wilson to drop out of law school but he continued his legal studies from his parents' home in Wilmington, North Carolina. After satisfying the examiners of his competence to practice law, he was admitted to the Georgia bar. For the next two years Wilson, in partnership with a fellow law graduate, set up a legal practice in Atlanta, the *de facto* capital of the South. The practice struggled to attract fee paying clients and closed after two years.

Manse to the White House

The failure of the enterprise can be put down to Wilson whose heart was not engaged in the irksome business of running a legal practice. Wilson was interested in legal history, constitutional law and jurisprudential philosophy – all academic subjects – but selling oneself to prospective clients and representing their interests in court had little appeal although such was the dearth of clients that Wilson only appeared in court on two or three occasions. In harsh reality, Wilson was not cut-out to be a legal practitioner.

After abandoning his short-lived legal career, Wilson enrolled with Johns Hopkins University to study government and history. In this ivy tower of learning Wilson flourished. At last he had found his métier Four years after enrolling, Wilson was awarded a postgraduate Ph.D degree. His doctoral thesis was titled *Congressional Government: A study in American Politics.* This was also his first published book in which he developed his conceptual ideas of reforming Congressional Government along British parliamentary lines. Since its publication, the book (which is still in print) has become a bible for students interested in the thorny issues inherent in a written constitution, whence the main powers of government are separated leading to the fragmentation of executive, legislative and judicial responsibility. This book was followed by several others in a similar constitutional vein. In 1902, Wilson published his *opus magnum: A History of the American People,* a work which ran to five volumes. In 1908 came *Constitutional Government in the United States* in which he developed further his reforming ideas propounded in *Congressional Government.* In this work he argued that the president of the United States is "the representative of no constituency but the whole people. When he speaks in his true character, he speaks of no special interest." Under a constitutional monarchy the head of state (ie king or queen) is not elected by the people, whereas under the American presidential system the head of state is elected to office following an election that makes it difficult, if not impossible, for the president to represent the whole of the country. Tensions arise where the incumbent president is seen to favour one section of the electorate over the other. Wilson's thesis that the president should represent the whole country is not a realistic one under the American constitutional model.

Armed with his post-graduate degree, Dr Woodrow Wilson joined the ranks of the professional academics by taking a post at Bryn Mawr College to teach young women history and political science. In 1888 he moved to Wesleyan University in Connecticut where he stayed for two years teaching constitutional law and politics. In 1890, at the age of thirty-three, Wilson received a call from Princeton University to take up the post of Professor of Jurisprudence and Political Economy. This proved to be a major turning point in Wilson's life. At Princeton, Wilson quickly established himself as the most popular faculty member, an inspiring teacher, and his remuneration reflected his senior status.

Twelve years after burnishing his credentials as a lecturer in constitutional law and politics, Dr Woodrow Wilson was unanimously elected the 13th president of Princeton University. For the next three years Wilson embarked on a radical program aimed at transforming Princeton into a university to rival Harvard and Yale. In three key areas Wilson's reforming agenda was successful. The intellectual footprint of the university was considerably expanded, academic standards were raised and its precarious financial state was placed on a firmer footing. But in two other key areas – democratizing and restructuring – Wilson's reforming zeal was not shared by a cohort of influential arch conservatives and wealthy alumni. His failure to secure these two key objectives almost brought Wilson to the point of resigning. Nonetheless, Wilson pressed on with his reforming agenda with varying degrees of success. It was during this time that Wilson's first love, politics, was re-awakened. In 1898, Wilson observed for the first time Congress in session; this stirred in him a latent longer for public service. About this time he formed a bond of friendship with Vice President Theodore Roosevelt whom he first met in the summer of 1902.

During the first decade of the new century, Wilson's desire for playing an active role in politics grew stronger. That opportunity came in 1910 when the bosses of the Democratic Party persuaded Wilson to run for governor of New Jersey. Having secured the Democratic Party nomination, Wilson fought the ensuing election in the manner of a seasoned campaigner, not the rookie he actually was. His boldest – and bravest – strategy was to distance himself from the party machine without whose support he would not have been nominated. Wilson was determined to show that he was no poodle of the party bosses.

The campaign afforded Wilson the opportunity to put to full use his oratorical skills honed over the years. His persuasive powers combined with a progressive agenda persuaded sufficient New Jersey voters to elect him to the governorship. During the final phase of the election campaign, Wilson was forced to step-down as president of Princeton University following pressure from the board of trustees. His forced resignation from the post of president took the gloss off his electoral triumph. But the resignation at least brought forward the transition from the professorial world of privilege and status into the arena of politics and public service.

Once in office, Wilson put into practice many of the (parliamentary) ideas set out in his book *Constitutional Government*. It was not long before the governor's reforming program caught the attention of voters beyond the state of New Jersey. Wilson's growing national reputation as a reformer was to propel him along a pathway leading to the Democratic presidential nomination and eventually to the White House.

Barely two years into the state governorship, Wilson believing that destiny had singled him out to be president threw his hat into the presidential ring. His friends and supporters raised $85,000 (adjusted for inflation that would be the equivalent of $2.4m today) to fund his presidential ambitions. At the contested Democratic Convention held in Baltimore, Maryland, Wilson secured the presidential nomination and campaigned on a program which stressed individualism, tariff reduction, banking and currency reform, stronger anti-trust laws, a federal income tax and state rights. In a three-way election held on November 5, 1912 in which the Republican Party was unable to unite behind one candidate, Wilson received less than fifty per cent of the popular vote but an overwhelming Electoral College vote. Had the Republican Party not been hopelessly split and had it fielded the popular and charismatic former President Theodore Roosevelt (who during the convention flounced off across town with his supporters to form a new Progressive Republican Party) instead of the excruciatingly dull incumbent President William Howard Taft, Wilson in all likelihood would not have gained the keys to the White House.

Following his inauguration Wilson got down to business with blistering pace and gusto; he steered through Congress a radical program of domestic reform mirroring his election campaign pledges apart from allowing the introduction of segregation between blacks and whites into federal departments. This policy of segregation was extremely controversial and went against the spirit of his election campaign. African Americans who voted for Wilson in large numbers became disillusioned and angry. To this day the black community has not forgotten nor forgiven his betrayal.

Wilson's main legislative achievements during his first term included tariff reform combined with a new tax regime oriented towards graduated federal income tax with less reliance being placed upon revenues derived from duties on imports; the creation of the Federal Reserve Board, a powerful agency charged with creating stability in the financial system and the economy through a government-controlled central bank (prior to the enactment the United States, unlike Britain and Germany, had no government-run central bank); the Clayton Anti-Trust Act which reinforced existing laws prohibiting anti-competitive business practices; and the Federal Trade Commission with powers to investigate corrupt and unfair business actions. In drawing up his legislative program, Wilson broke with tradition by appearing in person before the two houses of Congress and working in tandem with his party and cabinet. In this regard he was acting less like a president *primus sine pares* and more like a prime minster *primus inter-pares* under the British parliamentary model which he so admired.

These three major pieces of domestic legislation in the areas of banking, tariff and taxes and anti-trust are to this day the main pillars underpinning the world's largest economy – an enduring legacy bequeathed to the nation by a reforming, progressive president at the height of his powers.

The president's private study – desk replete with writing instruments, ink and a blotting pad

Wilson completed his first term by reforming child labour law (later struck down by the Supreme Court as being unconstitutional) and steering through Congress a package of pro-labour legislation.

The 1916 presidential election held on November 7 was a far tougher contest for the incumbent than the 1912 election. This time round the Republicans coalesced around a single candidate, Charles Evans Hughes, an associate justice of the Supreme Court who entered the contest as favourite.

By now the war in Europe was entering its third year and Wilson, who campaigned around the slogan "He Kept Us Out of War", secured a narrow majority in the Electoral College due in large part to winning the swing state of California.

Wilson's second term was dominated by the war in Europe and the threat to United States citizens and shipping posed by German U-boats.

Chapter Four

Falling in Love

"They were my salad days, when I was green in judgement." William
Shakespeare.

As a young man Woodrow Wilson was shy, diffident and awkward.
(Even in maturity Wilson was quite reserved and awkward in small
groups but supremely confident when addressing large gatherings.) As
far as is known he had no close female friends outside of his immediate
and extended family. In those days American co-educational colleges
were far from the norm, male and female students being segregated by
gender. Princeton University did not go co-educational until 1969 when
women undergraduates were admitted for the first time. While at
Princeton College, Wilson led, in his own words "a monastic life". He
was more interested in literature and debating politics, his two
favourite subjects, than pursuing romantic liaisons.

It was while reading law at Virginia University that Wilson fell madly in
love for the first time. The object of his affections was his younger
cousin, Hattie Woodrow, who lived in nearby Staunton. Hattie was by
all accounts an attractive, engaging nineteen year old with brown hair
and blue eyes. In observing the social conventions of the era the two
cousins corresponded with each other and met occasionally for walks
but it was not, in the terminology of the time, a courtship.

One night in September 1881, the two young cousins were partying
together when Wilson in a moment of impulsive idealization took
Hattie to one side and proposed marriage. Unfortunately, the young
man had completely misread his cousin's feelings towards him. His
love for her was not reciprocated. On the spot she rebuffed the proposal
of marriage. Wilson was devastated. He immediately left the party,
which was being held at his father's manse, and booked into a nearby
hotel. But instead of licking his wounds and drowning his sorrows at
the bar as most young men in the circumstances would have done, he
doubled down on his ill-fated proposal of marriage by composing a
note to Hattie imploring her to change her mind. But Hattie was made

Falling in Love

of sterner stuff; his exhortation fell on deaf ears but to spare his feelings she rejected the marriage proposal on the grounds that they were too closely related. Unrequited love is invariably hard to come to terms with at any time of life but for a young incurable romantic it was a terrible blow. Throughout his life Wilson was an inveterate accumulator of correspondence but Hattie's letters to him were an exception such was the pain of rejection.

Less than two years after being rejected by Hattie (and according to some sources by other young women as well), the luckless Wilson had fallen in love again. The lady upon whom Wilson had set his sights was Ellen Louise Axson, the pretty twenty-two year old daughter of Reverend Samuel Edward Axson, a Presbyterian minister. Ellen's mother, sadly, had recently died and it had fallen upon her daughter to take care of both her father, who was suffering from depression, and her two younger brothers. At such a young age that was quite a burden to carry.

If the young man was to win the heart of Ellen in the marriage stakes, he would have to raise his game for Ellen had already rejected three marriage proposals from suitors. Clearly, she was a discerning young woman when it came to choosing a marriage partner. Wilson was not the handsomest of fellows, nor at the time did he play any college sports which would have broadened his appeal. By now he had taken to wearing his trademark pince-nez style spectacles giving him the appearance of an elderly clergyman peering over the pulpit at the congregation below. Not quite an image a fashionable young woman with an artistic bent would find attractive. But Wilson had no cause to worry. Unlike Ellen's other suitors, Wilson had an intellectual hinterland and that was more important to Ellen than pure looks or sporting prowess alone. It was almost love at first sight for both of them. Five months after their first meeting, the young couple were engaged but had to postpone their wedding due to the worsening medical condition of Ellen's father who, tragically, committed suicide while hospitalized for depression.

The wedding eventually took place in Savannah, Georgia on

Ellen Louise Axson, a Presbyterian minister's daughter who married Woodrow Wilson

Falling in Love

June 24, 1885. The groom was twenty-eight years of age and his bride twenty-five. For the newly weds it was a marriage made in Heaven. The happy couple complemented each other perfectly and Wilson was welcomed whole heartedly into the Axson family. Ellen's younger brother, Stockton Axson, many years later recalled that Wilson "was so very cordial that I lost my heart to him at once". Throughout his life, Woodrow Wilson had few close male friends – they could be counted on one hand. But Stockton would over time become Wilson's closest male friend, a friendship that was to last a lifetime. Wilson was not by nature a chummy or clubbable person preferring the companionship of intelligent, uncritical, empathetic women over men.

Ellen and Woodrow had three children together, all daughters. Margaret was the first born; she was the spitting image of her father even down to wearing similar spectacles, musically gifted, never married. Later in life she developed an interest in Hinduism eventually settling in India where she joined a mystic sect. She died in her adopted country during the Second World War at the relatively young age of fifty-seven. Jessie, the second born daughter, had blond hair and large blue eyes and possessed a finely chiselled face. She was the prettiest of the three siblings, also the most religious, a political activist and along with Margaret an advocate of women's suffrage. She died at the age of forty-five while undergoing abdominal surgery. Eleanor (also known as Nell or Nellie) was the last born and reputedly her father's favourite. Her dark hair complemented her dark eyes. Eleanor had a light-hearted approach to life; she married, much to the displeasure of her parents, a fifty-year old widower with seven children, namely William Gibbs McAdoo who held the post of secretary of treasury in her father's administration. The marriage did not prosper and was eventually dissolved. Eleanor outlived her siblings by two decades. She died in 1967 aged seventy-seven.

Often referred to as the "surrogate daughter" of the Wilsons, Helen Woodrow Bones was the first cousin of Woodrow Wilson. Her mother, Marion Woodrow, was the sister of Wilson's mother, Jessie. The three Wilson daughters and their cousin Helen were inseparable during their

Jessie Woodrow Wilson Sayre who died aged forty-five while undergoing abdominal surgery.

Falling in Love

formative years. In 1914, following the death of Ellen Wilson, Helen moved into the White House as Wilson's private secretary and carried out certain official duties normally undertaken by the first lady.

Woodrow and Ellen had, apart from one period of instability, a happy and deeply satisfying marriage. The couple adored each other and whenever apart they would keep up an almost constant stream of affectionate correspondence. Throughout their marriage, Ellen would take a keen interest in whatever project her husband was undertaking at the time, always there to offer objective advice or provide emotional support but never usurping him. She was comfortable within the family circle – providing a safe harbour to shelter her family from the political storms that often razed round her husband. She understood how he ticked and there were no dark corners of his life that she did not have access to. Her leisure time was devoted to drawing and painting and as first lady she endeavoured to improve the housing conditions of African Americans living in slums lining the alleyways of the nation's capital.

Ellen had inherited from her father the melancholy gene that at times of stress would cause her to slip into a silent world of her own where she was "unreachable and beyond comfort". Over time she would come out of her depressive state and life would resume as before. During these melancholic episodes, Ellen would encourage her husband to holiday alone either in England or the British island of Bermuda.

It was while holidaying in Bermuda in 1907 that Wilson met by chance Mrs Mary Hulbert Peck, a middle-aged, chain-smoking, society hostess who had since 1892 sojourned during the winter months on the island with her only son who suffered from poor health. Mrs Peck was born Mary Allen and in 1883 married Thomas Harbach Hulbert, a mining engineer, who died following an accident in 1889. A year later Mary Hulbert married Thomas Dowse Peck, a wealthy woollen merchant of Pittsfield, Massachusetts. The marriage did not prosper and ended in divorce. Mrs Peck was not by any stretch of the imagination a *femme fatale* but she was charming, vivacious, witty, well-read and had a talent for casting her fun-loving spell over men. Mark Twain and the

Falling in Love

Governor of Bermuda together with a cast of the great and the good of the island dined at her table. She numbered amongst her circle of acquaintances Rudyard Kipling and his wife. Wilson was immediately captivated by this tall, party-going woman from Pittsfield, Massachusetts.

The following year Wilson took his bicycle over to Bermuda and once again met Mary Hulbert Peck. And so began a flirtatious relationship that was to last for many years. Wilson would accompany Mrs Peck to tea dances (not that Wilson danced) and dinner parties. The couple would take long walks along the South Shore occasionally stopping so Wilson could read to his *mon amoureuse* his favourite poems from the *Oxford Book of English Verse*. There was nothing clandestine about their friendship. Wilson openly talked about Mrs Peck to Ellen and often invited her to the family home. Likewise Mrs Peck would invite the Wilsons to her home in Pittsfield. Mary and Ellen would go on shopping trips together. Mrs Peck maintained an apartment in New York (which she shared with her mother and son) where Wilson would meet his friend without Ellen. The Metropolitan Museum of Art was one public place the two friends visited together.

There has been much speculation by Wilson's biographers and others as to whether the relationship was a sexual one or merely platonic. On Wilson's part it was a profoundly emotional relationship from which he was unable to extricate himself until he married his second wife, Edith. From 1908 until 1915 there flowed between the two friends an almost constant stream of letters which Wilson addressed to "My precious one, my beloved Mary". Although the letters – two hundred or more– were never sexually explicit, they were nonetheless highly intimate in which Wilson poured out his heart. In Wilson's own words, "more warm than discreet". Wilson unashamedly used Mary Peck as an anvil upon which he hammered out his innermost thoughts and feelings.

From the outset Ellen suspected that her husband was in an inappropriate relationship with a married woman. She reprimanded her husband on the eve of his departure for a cycling tour of England in

Falling in Love

"God has stricken me almost beyond what I can bear." Woodrow Wilson writing to Mary Hulbert (formerly Mrs Mary Peck).

1908 which left Wilson distraught. In the end Ellen seems to have forgiven her husband for his infidelities and indiscretions and for the unhappiness he had caused her.

Shortly after Wilson won the 1913 presidential election, he took Ellen and two of their daughters to Bermuda in order to rest and come to terms with the onerous duties that awaited him upon his inauguration. Green Cove Cottage where the Wilson family stayed was situated on a secluded peninsula overlooking the sea and surrounded by a high wall which kept snooping photographers and reporters at bay. The cottage was in the possession of Mary Peck. During Wilson's first term, the first lady invited Mrs Peck to be a weekend guest at the White House. Clearly Ellen had saintly qualities that set her apart from the sisterhood of married women.

Apart from depression, Ellen's physical condition had for a number of years been deteriorating. She was suffering from what in those days the doctors termed Bright's disease. Two physicians were consulted and they found Ellen had tuberculosis of the kidneys so far advanced as to be incurable. Kidney failure can result in premature death (nowadays the disease is treatable). During the seventeen months as first lady, Ellen's health worsened and on August 6, 1914 with her family at her bedside and her husband holding her hand she slipped away. Wilson was overwhelmed with grief. He wept uncontrollably. "Oh my God, what am I to do?" Wilson's grief was so deep that for a time he could bear to speak of Ellen even to his daughters. When at last he was able to talk to them he confided, "She was so radiant.....So happy! We must so grateful for her sake that she did not see the world crash into ruin. It would have broken her heart."

Falling in Love

Over in Europe the land armies of Germany, Great Britain and France were being mobilized and within days of Ellen's death all three countries were at war. These were the darkest days of Wilson's life and his soul-mate of thirty years was no longer at his side. Years later when Wilson was approaching the end of his own life he confided in his youngest daughter, Eleanor: "I owe everything to your mother – you know that don't you?" After talking about their lives together, Eleanor turned to her father "I wish I could hand her torch to my own children." "You can – tell them about her. That is enough."

In one sense the war in Europe and the affect it was having on the United States – the New York Stock Exchange was in free-fall, heavy selling of the dollar was taking place, trade with Europe was disrupted due to the naval blockade of Germany imposed by the Royal Navy – was for Wilson a blessing in disguise for it left him with little time to grieve for his beloved Ellen. Helen Woodrow Bones along with Margaret Wilson took over some of the duties previously undertaken by the first lady.

On entering the White House, Wilson was introduced to Captain Cary Travers Grayson, a surgeon in the United States Navy who had been assigned by ex-president William Taft to look after the health of the incoming president. Wilson and Dr Grayson became firm friends and played golf together. Grayson, who at the time was courting a young lady who lived in New York, was concerned that Helen Bones did not have a social life. The doctor and his New York girl friend had a mutual friend who lived in Washington DC – Edith Bolling Galt, a forty-two year old vivacious widow, financially independent, an adventurous traveller. Grayson arranged for Helen to meet Edith Galt. The two women hit it off immediately. They had much in common and would take long walks together returning to the White House in Edith's little electric automobile.

One afternoon in March, Helen invited Edith back to the White House for tea, the two women having been on a muddy walk together. The two friends took the elevator to the second floor and as they were walking along the

Falling in Love

Edith Bolling Galt driving her electric automobile in 1904. She was the first woman to hold a driving licence in Washington DC.

hallway they came face to face with the president and Dr Cary Grayson, the two gentlemen having just returned from a round of golf. All four had shoes covered in mud. Edith being tall with a shapely figure immediately caught Wilson's nautical eye. He liked the cut of her jib. He was smitten by this strikingly attractive woman. With Helen acting as a chaperone (at the time it went against established convention for a newly widowed man to be seen with an eligible woman without another woman present) Woodrow and Edith would dine and take rides together in the presidential limousine. As the weeks passed the relationship between the president and Edith Bolling Galt grew closer. Hardly a day went by when Edith did not receive an affectionate letter from Wilson (Woodrow had form when it came to epistolary). He was desperate to marry Edith at the earliest opportunity but convention decreed that remarriage could not take place within twelve months of the death of one's spouse. Wilson certainly found his new friend sexually attractive. It is open to speculation whether Wilson's base instincts were reciprocated. Wilson was still in his fifties and according to one source had a healthy libido. However, their relationship did not rest on pure physical attraction alone. Their backgrounds and religious faith were in many respects similar. Edith was born in Wytheville, Virginia in 1872; her father was a local judge and a blood descendant of Pocahontas, a native American woman who married John Rolfe, the first English settler in Virginia. Before the Civil War, the Bolling family owned a number of plantations worked by slaves. With the abolition of slavery, the Bollings, whilst not reduced to penury, lost much of their acquired wealth.

Edith was one of eleven children, two of whom died in infancy. She received a fairly basic education, primarily at home. According to one of Wilson's biographers her hand writing was "primitive...almost illegible". From childhood Edith was quite judgmental and once she formed an opinion she asserted it with boldness and stuck with it through thick and thin. Everything was either black or white with no shades in between. The word "nuance" did not figure in her lexicon.

Edith attended church regularly and became a life-long member of the Episcopalian Church. In 1896 Edith married Norman Galt whose family owned a high-end jewellery store within a stone's throw of the White House. The Galts had one son who, sadly, died a few days after being born. The birth was traumatic and Edith was unable to bear further children. Norman Galt died in 1908 leaving Edith a substantial inheritance. Now wealthy and independent Edith travelled extensively

Edith Bolling

both in her homeland and abroad. It was while travelling through Europe, Edith acquired a penchant for wearing expensive clothes designed by a renowned Paris milliner.

Edith Bolling was born into an upper-class Southern family

After a whirl-wind courtship and with the blessing of Wilson's three daughters, Edith became the president's second wife on December 18, 1915, sixteen months after Ellen had been buried in her home town of Rome, Georgia.

The newly wed first lady showed little interest in politics as, indeed, she had done throughout her life. Often she would be present when her husband was reading confidential papers relating to the war and in the same room when he met his advisors on government business but during the early years of their marriage she never sought to interfere in state affairs – that situation was to change dramatically in the last eighteen months of her husband's presidency.

Edith idolized her second husband. Wilson for his part was no longer the sad and lonely figure aimlessly wandering the corridors of the White House as he mourned the loss of Ellen. Edith gave him a new lease of life at a crucial time when the whole world was looking to America and its president to bring the ghastly war in Europe to an end.

Chapter Five

Lake District Summers

"There is no spot in the world in which I am so completely at rest and peace as in the lake country." Woodrow Wilson in a letter to his wife, Ellen.

Woodrow Wilson was in his fortieth year when he first ventured outside his homeland. On May 30, 1896, after much hesitation, he boarded in New York the *Ethiopia,* an ocean steamer belonging to the Anchor Line *en route* to her home port of Glasgow. Wilson was travelling alone. During the months leading up to his departure for Britain, Wilson had been in poor health brought on by stress and overwork. In May 1896, Wilson, although it was not diagnosed as such at the time, suffered a small stroke which left him with a numbness in the tips of several fingers and an inability to write with his right hand (he deployed his left hand to write letters until regaining the ability to write with his right). His physicians prescribed a period of rest from his onerous duties at Princeton. Ellen felt that a two-month vacation in England would restore his health but she would not accompany him preferring to stay at home to look after the children and manage his affairs while he was away. Reluctantly, Wilson agreed to visit Britain without his soul mate at his side.

During the Atlantic crossing Wilson met a married couple from South Carolina – Judge Charles Woods and his wife – who were planning a cycling tour of the Scottish Lowlands and England. The Woods invited Wilson to join them. Wilson had been a late convert to the pleasures of cycling (or wheeling as he called it) having taken up the sport around 1894. On June 11, the *Ethiopia* docked at Glasgow – not far from the town of Paisley where Wilson's maternal grandfather, Thomas Woodrow, had been a Congregational Church minister before relocating to Carlisle in England in 1820.

Before setting off on his cycling odyssey with the Woods, Wilson had some university business – assigned to him by Princeton – to conduct in Edinburgh and Cambridge. He returned to Glasgow on June 24. The cyclists' first objective was the historic coastal town of Ayr where they stayed overnight. From Ayr the trio cycled to the border town of Dumfries leaving on the morning of June 27. Later that day they crossed into England arriving in Carlisle in time for an evening meal. Wilson spent two days in Carlisle in what turned out to be a futile search to find the childhood home of his mother, Jessie.

Disappointed that he was unable to find his ancestral home, Wilson without his two cycling companions (who had stayed behind in Carlisle to repair one of their bicycles) boarded a train for the northern Lake District town of Keswick. From Keswick, Wilson mounted his "dromedary" and headed south for the village of Rydal where he had arranged to rendezvous with the Woods. The road to Rydal passes alongside a serpentine stretch of water known as the Thirlmere Reservoir (the reservoir provides Manchester – 90 miles away – with fresh water and had only recently been constructed following strenuous opposition from conservationists).

Beyond the reservoir the road to Rydal becomes progressively steeper as it climbs towards the mountain pass of Dunmail Raise, a geological fault between high fells. Wilson was riding a single speed bicycle (bicycles with gears were not commercially available at the time) and may well have found this section of the road strenuous. The physical exertion required to reach the top of the pass is rewarded with a bird's eye view of the beautiful vale of Grasmere stretching across the glacial floor below the pass. An 18th-century writer described the scene as an "unsuspected paradise"; and so it must have seemed to Wilson as he gathered speed on the downhill section of the road leading to Rydal via the village of Grasmere, the epicentre of "Wordsworth Country".

On entering Grasmere – described by its most famous resident as "the most loveliest spot that man hath found" – Wilson made a beeline for

Dove Cottage, Grasmere

Lake District Summers

Dove Cottage, the former home of William Wordsworth and his talented sister, Dorothy. It was while residing at the 17th-century cottage that Wordsworth wrote some of his best works. After inspecting the interior of the famous rustic cottage, Wilson cycled the short distance to Rydal Mount where the great romantic poet lived from 1813 until his death in 1850.

Although now open to the public, Rydal Mount at the time of Wilson's visit in 1896 was in private ownership and he had to contend with picking a tiny flower from a wall close to Wordsworth's last home. This he enclosed with a letter to Ellen describing the route he had just cycled from Keswick to Rydal as "16 enchanting miles". Wilson had fallen in love with this unique and beguiling corner of England which over the next decade he would return time and time again. Even in the final phase of his life, twenty-two years after his first visit, he was planning a vacation with his family in Grasmere. Sadly, due to serious illness the planned visit never came to pass.

The following day Wilson continued his exploration of the area visiting *Nab Cottage* where Thomas De Quincey once lodged and *Fox How,* the home of Dr Thomas Arnold, a contemporary of William Wordsworth and the father of the poet, Matthew Arnold.

For those of a literary disposition or, indeed, anyone who is plain curious no visit to Grasmere is complete without visiting the Wordsworth family grave in the churchyard of St Oswald's which lies above the banks of the River Rothay. Next to the grave of William and his wife Mary lies the grave of their daughter, Dora.

After paying his respects at the grave of his literary idol, Wilson rejoined the Woods at Rydal from where the trio made their way to the railway station at Windermere for their onward train journey to York. From York, Wilson cycled 200 miles to London (whether he cycled the whole way to London, which would be quite a stretch, or hopped onto a train for part of the journey is not recorded). In London he visited the

Lake District Summers

Palace of Westminister home to the Government of Great Britain and Ireland (since 1922, the United Kingdom of Great Britain and Northern Ireland).

During his summer tour of England, Woodrow also found time to visit the university town of Oxford which he found delightful. He was enthralled by the quads and gardens of the colleges. From Oxford he made his way to Somerset in the south-west corner of England. He was heading for the ancient market town of Langport to pay his respects to yet another English-born admirer of his, the constitutional writer Walter Bagehot who died in 1877 and whose grave lies in the churchyard of All Saints.

At the end of August, Wilson returned to Glasgow to board his steamship for the return leg of his journey back to New York.

Three years after his first visit to Great Britain, Wilson returned for a second cycling tour of the Lake District accompanied on this occasion by his brother-in-law, Stockton Axson, who held the post of professor of English at Princeton. The duo crossed the Atlantic on another steamship owned by the Anchor Line named *Furnessia*. Wilson preferred the Anchor Line to other transatlantic operators as their vessels were small and slow, thus prolonging the passage which he regarded as a bonus as he enjoyed his time at sea.

The *Furnessia* docked in Glasgow on July 4, 1899. Once again Ellen stayed behind to look after the children. Wilson was in need of a rest from his onerous professorial duties at Princeton which were adversely affecting his physical and mental well-being. In his memoirs, Professor Axson admitted that he too "had been pretty badly run down" and so greatly appreciated his brother-in-law's "gentleness and consideration of this tour". Instead of riding inordinately long distances as Wilson had done during his 1896 tour of Great Britain, the two Princetonians travelled by train for the major part of their tour with their bicycles stored in the luggage van until required.

Lake District Summers

"The most beautiful road in the world." Wilson writing to Ellen on his second tour of the Lake District in 1899.

After disembarking, Wilson and his brother-in-law boarded a train for Edinburgh where they had according to Axson "two or three most delightful days" before returning to Glasgow to begin a literary cycling tour of Robert Burns' country starting in Alloway, the birthplace of the National Bard of Scotland. The tour ended in Dumfries where the great poet died at the tender age of thirty-seven. On July 8, the two professors boarded a train bound for Penrith in England where they took to their "wheels".

For their joint tour of Britain, Wilson and his brother-in-law had acquired two new bicycles – a shaft-driven Columbia model for which each paid $75, a king's ransom at the time. For such a hefty price the bicycles, surprisingly, had no mudguards unlike English models.

Rydal Water

Lake District Summers

On Saturday, July 8, the duo set off to explore the Ullswater Valley set amongst a line of friendly fells between Pooley Bridge in the north and Patterdale in the south. The valley is dominated by Ullswater, a dog-legged lake of exceptionally clear water, the second largest in the Lake District after Windermere. To many connoisseurs, Ullswater is the most beautiful of all the lakes in the region, the northern end of which is flanked by rounded green hills of modest height, whereas, in stark contrast, its southern head is girdled by deeply indented fells and mountains.

To school children the world over golden daffodils and the shores of Ullswater are synonymous.

I wandered lonely as a cloud,
That floats on high o'er vales and hill,
When all at once I saw a crowd,
A host of golden daffodils,
Beside the lake, beneath the trees,
Fluttering and dancing in the breeze.

Ullswater

Lake District Summers

When the cycling duo passed the spot close to the lake shore which inspired William Wordsworth to write the most famous lines of poetry in the English language the "fluttering and dancing" daffodils were no longer in season.

Wilson and his brother-in-law spent Saturday night at the White Lion Inn in the small village of Patterdale near the head of Ullswater. Woodrow in a mood of elation told Ellen that the road alongside Ullswater "must surely be the most beautiful road in the world" and that the pair had had "the most perfect day....with its keen fresh air out of the West, its intense sunlight and quick moving shadows, showing every peak and line of the mountains, every sloping shore, every home, or group of trees or herd of cattle in a light chosen for the picture. No light seems ever to be too keen or bright. There is always a soft suffusion and touch of mystery. The northern end of the lake lies between hills that rise with a soft slope to no great height; but the scenery grows bolder and grander at every turn of the way ......until it becomes magnificent.....It is all the more perfect a road because its beauty seems, not deliberate but inevitable."

Wilson was an extraordinary gifted wordsmith. His evocative description of the beautiful Ullswater Valley is a remarkable piece of perceptive writing – "keen fresh air out of the West" "intense sunlight and quick moving shadows" "a soft suffusion and touch of mystery" – capture the very essence of Lakeland.

The next day the two intrepid cyclists doubled-back along the valley towards Pooley Bridge before setting a westerly course for Keswick (the exact route is not recorded but it was probably via the settlement of Dockray). They spent four nights at the George Hotel in Keswick – longer than intended due to the inclement weather. The enforced stayover allowed them to inspect Greta Hall, the one-time home of the romantic poet Robert Southey and his grave in the churchyard of Crosthwaite, a village on the northern fringe of Keswick. Southey was a close friend of William Wordsworth and a member of the group known as the 'Lake Poets'. Wordsworth penned an epitaph to his friend which Woodrow and Stockton read on a memorial plaque inside Crosthwaite Church. The duo also found time to climb a small wooded hill known as Castle Head. On topping the hill the pair sat "enchanted.....all the exquisite length and breadth and setting of Derwentwater" could be seen, Wilson later recorded.

On July 10, the explorers took to their "wheels" in search of the house where William Wordsworth was born in 1770. They cycled alongside Bassenthwaite Water – "a ride to remember" he later told Ellen – and in the ancient market town of Cockermouth, which lies at the confluence of the rivers Cocker and Derwent, they found the former home of Wordsworth which today is a Grade I listed building in the care of the National Trust. The two cyclists returned to Keswick by train. (Nowadays that would not be possible as the line was closed to passengers in 1966 at the behest of Dr Richard Beeching, a former chairman of British Railways, who managed to do what the *Luftwaffe* failed to achieve in 1940: the decimation of the transport structure of rural Britain – an egregious act of rural vandalism for which the nation now laments).

By July 13, the inclement weather gave way to "glorious sunshine" allowing the "two pilgrims" (not the author's description but Wilson's) to mount their cycles and head off in the direction of "Wordsworth Country", thus retracing the route taken by Woodrow in his 1896 tour of the Lake District. Wilson was keen to show his brother-in-law *Dove Cottage* and all the other shrines associated with the philosophical poet.

After inspecting *Dove Cottage,* the "two pilgrims" signed the visitors' book – Wilson for the second time and his brother-in-law for the first. Stockton later wrote:

We went to the arbor which is described by Wordsworth in his famous poem on Dove Cottage, a poem which I have heard Mr Wilson read again and again, always with tears in his eyes, it being among the things that for a time at least he loved most in the poetry of Wordsworth. The whole region delighted him out of measure, partly for its own beauty, partly for its association with the serene poet who has meant so much to him.

The poem that brought tears to Wilson's eyes is titled *A Farewell*.

St Oswald's Church, Grasmere wherein the churchyard above the banks of the River Rothay lie the graves of the Wordsworths

From Dove Cottage, the Princetonians cycled a few miles along the lakeside road to Ambleside via Rydal Mount. Ambleside, a former mill town whose buildings are predominantly built of locally-mined dark grey slate, lies close to the northern head of Windermere where the Romans built their fort of *Galava* overlooking the lake. Ambleside is surrounded by a cluster of fells, less dramatic than those that overlook Coniston or Keswick but nonetheless stunningly beautiful. When

Lake District Summers

Woodrow and Stockton rolled into Ambleside in 1899, they would have found a charming quiet town where cotton, corn, paper and bobbin mills formed the bedrock of its economy. Today Ambleside is the nation's go-to place for outdoor clothing and footwear. It is one of the most popular places in Lakeland and during public and school holidays is over-run with tourists. The duo stayed two nights at the White Lion Inn in Ambleside. Their intention was to cycle to Coniston and Hawkshead but Stockton, whose health was not particularly robust, was brought low by an attack of appendicitis. Plans were changed and on Saturday the "two pilgrims" departed for the railway station at Windermere where they boarded a train for Durham. Wilson in a letter to Ellen wrote that her brother's attack of appendicitis in Ambleside had prevented them from carrying out the program there. But he was still grateful for having seen more of the Lake District then in 1896 and felt he had "nothing to regret".

The college professors spent three days in Durham where they attended a service at the great cathedral founded in 1093. Their visit coincided with the *court of assizes. The visiting judge was Sir William Grantham, an eminent High Court judge from London who was presiding over a murder trial. Wilson and his brother-in-law spent a day in court observing how the court's criminal procedures differed from those in their home country.

From Durham "the pilgrims" resumed their tour of England by visiting the cathedral cities in the east of England and the university towns of Cambridge and Oxford. Stockton then went on to Surrey to stay with an American friend, whilst Woodrow took a ferry over to Ireland. His paternal grandparents came from County Tyrone, part of what is now Northern Ireland. His visit to Ireland is sketchily recorded but there is a presumption that he and his bicycle made it to Belfast and substantive evidence that he visited the port of Drogheda in the historic county of Louth. It is a matter of conjecture whether Wilson visited Dublin (35 miles south of Drogheda) although there is no record of him venturing as far as the fair city.

*All courts of assizes have been abolished; the criminal jurisdiction of assizes is exercised today by the Crown Court.

The "two pilgrims" met up again in Glasgow for their return voyage to New York. They were booked on the same ocean liner that brought them across the Atlantic but at Stockton's request they transferred their bookings to a larger, faster vessel sailing earlier. The *City of Rome* was a four-mastered, four-funnelled white elephant of a ship that on the voyage across to New York nearly suffered the same fate as the *Titanic*. According to Axson – and his account is supported by the captain's log – the ship hit an iceberg in fog. "The *City of Rome* had a cutter bow enabling her," in the words of Stockton, "to slide up onto the shelf like a sled. The shelf broke and let us back into the water but more on our side than on our keel." With one exception all the passengers faced the possibility that the ship would go down. Wilson, according to his brother-in-law, was unperturbed by the incident. During the period of mortal danger he was chatting to a Presbyterian preacher from New York "in the most natural way as if going up on icebergs was a daily experience and an event of no concern whatsoever". The *City of Rome* was scrapped shortly afterwards.

It is pointless to speculate (although it doesn't stop the author from so doing) what the geopolitical consequences might have been had the *City of Rome* not survived the encounter with the iceberg. Had Wilson not lived to become the 28th president of the United States would America have entered the First World War earlier, or later, or not at all? If the latter would Germany have defeated Great Britain and France and, if so, what shape would the eventual peace settlement have taken? The terms imposed on Russia by the Brest-Litovsk Treaty were draconian in the extreme. Would Great Britain and France have been treated any more favourably?

After a lapse of three years Woodrow Wilson was back in Britain and on this occasion accompanied by his wife. Their three children were growing up fast and old enough to be left in the care of friends. Since the encounter with the iceberg, Wilson's academic career had moved up a gear or two. In June 1902, he was unanimously elected president of Princeton University. Husband and wife sailed across the Atlantic on the *Oceanic* and after disembarking at Liverpool they took a train to Chester. From the old Roman town, Woodrow and Ellen boarded a train for the Furness area of Lancashire (that part of the historic county of Lancashire lying north of Morecambe Bay). Woodrow was keen to show Ellen Furness Abbey which was founded in 1123 by the Cistercians. The old abbey – or what remains of it after Henry VIII ordered its destruction as an act of revenge because the pope would not annul his first marriage to Katherine of Aragon so he could marry Anne Boleyn – is situated in a lovely vale close to the not so lovely ship building town of Barrow. The abbey is a worthy tourist destination in its own right, especially if the visitor is interested in monastic architecture. The remains are impressive but for Woodrow and Ellen their primary interest was poetic for the abbey inspired William Wordsworth to compose the poem *At Furness Abbey*.

*Of the day's journey was too distant far
For any cautious man, a Structure famed
Beyond its neighbourhood, the antique
Walls Of that large Abbey which within the
vale of Nightshade, to St. Mary's honour
built, Stands yet, a mouldering Pile, with
fractured Arch, Belfry, and Images, and
living Trees, A holy Scene!*

Furness Abbey

Lake District Summers

"No doubt God could have made a lovelier country than this Lake District but I cannot believe he ever did." Wilson writing to his friend, Robert Bridges in 1906.

The Wilsons were following in the footsteps of Queen Victoria who visited the abbey in 1845 with her lady-in-waiting. During the 19th-century the abbey was popular with those of a literary and artistic bent.

From Furness Abbey, the Wilsons made their way to Ambleside and thence to Grasmere where they had booked a room at the Rothay Hotel (now the Wordsworth Hotel) situated in the centre of the village. The couple stayed seven nights at the hotel which is within walking distance of *Dove Cottage* and *Rydal Mount* and the other Wordsworthian shrines that meant so much to them. Ellen was, if anything, an even greater admirer of the works of William Wordsworth than her husband and her knowledge of his poetry was at least equal to his.

During their sojourn at Grasmere, the Wilsons went by horse-drawn conveyance to Ullswater via the high-level Kirkstone Pass. At the top of the pass stands the highest inn in Lakeland where the couple stopped for refreshments. From the inn their conveyance took them over the pass to Ullswater where at Glenridding they boarded a steam yacht that took them on a scenic tour of the lake – the same lake which three years earlier had made such a marked impression on Woodrow when he and Stockton cycled its full length.

After checking-out of their hotel, the Wilsons moved on to Keswick from where they toured the north-western area of the Lake District taking in Buttermere and Crummock Water, two beautiful lakes which on a smaller scale encapsulates the intrinsic beauty of Lakeland. While in Keswick, Woodrow took the opportunity to show his wife Crosthwaite Church and the grave of Robert Southey. Ellen, too, had fallen under the spell of this exquisite corner of England with its spectacular landscape and its associations with William Wordsworth and the other Lake Poets. Just like her husband, Ellen was well and truly hooked.

Lake District Summers

Windermere as seen from Loughrigg Fell

On July 18, the Wilsons departed Keswick for Edinburgh before returning to England for a tour of its historic cathedral towns. On August 24, Woodrow and Ellen embarked on a four-week tour of continental Europe starting in Paris.

Refreshed and reinvigorated after his summer vacation in Europe, Wilson once more threw himself into reforming Princeton against concerted opposition from troublesome colleagues, recalcitrant trustees and Princeton's rich and influential alumni. Wilson's ultimate objective was to remodel Princeton along the lines of Oxford and Cambridge with their quads and gardens enclosed by college buildings. The constant battles over his reform program eventually took a heavy toll on the president's health. In May 1906, Wilson woke to find that he had lost the sight in his left eye caused by a blood clot. Although it was not diagnosed as such at the time modern medical knowledge would point to Wilson having suffered a stroke. Wilson sought medical advice from three specialists, one of whom recommended that he should take a period of rest from his onerous duties at Princeton. Where better to convalesce, reasoned Ellen, then her husband's "beloved Lake District". Previous visits to the English lakes had done wonders for his health following illness brought on by overwork. So Ellen and Woodrow decided to spend the summer in "Wordsworth Country" But this time they would take their three daughters with them.

Instead of staying in hotels as Woodrow and Ellen had done on their previous visit to England, the Wilsons decided to rent a cottage for the duration of their stay. On July 10, 1906, the family settled into Loughrigg Cottage at Rydal. Wilson in a letter to a friend remarked: "It is most picturesque and delightfully situated, close by Rothay stream and under the shadow of Loughrigg, and though we are a tight fit, I am sure we shall be most comfortable and happy in it. It is at the heart of the region we most love."

Loughrigg is a fell of modest height overlooking four lakes – Rydal Water, Windermere, Grasmere and Elter Water. The "stream" is the River Rothay which rises close to the summit of Dunmail Raise – the mountain pass Wilson cycled over during his first and second tour of the region – and merges into the River Brathay south-west of Ambleside before their combined waters disappear completely into the northern depths of Windermere.

A little upstream from Loughrigg Cottage stands a charming three-arched stone bridge which spans the River Rothay. The bridge standing in a parkland setting is centuries old and is known as Pelter Bridge. Shortly after settling into his holiday cottage, Woodrow was crossing Pelter Bridge when he was befriended by Frederick Yates, a charismatic local artist "with a handsome rugged face and thick tousled hair". The two gentlemen struck up a conversation during which Yates declared: "We're poor, but thank God, not respectable." This statement of impropriety apparently bemused Wilson who for years afterwards enjoyed recounting it to others when the subject of their first meeting came up.

Loughrigg Cottage, Rydal where the Wilson family stayed in the summer of 1906

The River Rothay at Pelter Bridge, Rydal

Lake District Summers

Frederick (Fred) Yates was born in Southampton in 1854. Shortly after his birth his family moved to Liverpool. Yates had a natural talent for painting. His art education included a spell at the Paris studios of renowned French painters. In 1886 he moved to California to teach art. Shortly after arriving in California, Yates met and married Emily, a music teacher born in New Haven, Connecticut.

In 1890, Fred and Emily moved to England where their daughter, Mary (who was to become a talented artist in her own right) was born. Shortly after moving back to England, Yates (who by now had acquired an international reputation as a portraitist) had received a commission to paint the educationalist Miss Charlotte Mason who had settled in Ambleside. Like many artists before and since, Yates fell in love with the unspoilt beauty of the Lake District and decided to relocate there with his family. They rented a cottage in Rydal, a short distance from the Wilsons' holiday home.

According to Wilson's daughter, Eleanor: "It was a case of friendship at first sight, although they were unlike in many respects. Fred Yates was an artist, delightfully uninhibited, careless in his appearance, unversed in world affairs. Yet the painter and the college president had also much in common. They both loved poetry, humanity, all forms of beauty, and laughter. Each had a devoted artist wife. Both were idealists." And so began a friendship that was to endure until the death of Fred Yates in 1919. So close was their friendship that Wilson invited Yates to attend his inauguration as 28th president of the United States and as his special guest at the White House dinner following the inauguration ceremony. As a mark of their friendship, Wilson gave his English friend the inaugural flag as a souvenir. According to one source the flag was the one that Woodrow Wilson rested his hand on while taking his oath of office although it may well have been one of the five huge flags adorning the West Front of the Capitol on the day of the inauguration.

During the course of their stay at Loughrigg Cottage the Wilsons would invite Fred Yates and his family over for tea. According to

Lake District Summers

*Andrew Wilson in his book *A President's Love Affair with the Lake District*, "Yates gave Ellen painting lessons and made portraits of all five Wilsons." Eleanor later recorded: "While Ellen sketched, Woodrow and his daughters explored the lovely valleys and mountains on foot or in slow-moving ancient charabancs, coming back to the cottage in time for high tea by the fire. In the evening Woodrow taught the girls to play [the card game of] whist. Every Sunday they walked together to church. There was only one mishap to mar an idyllic summer, Nellie had the German measles." Later on in the holiday, Wilson would sit for Fred Yates who had been commissioned by Princeton University to paint a full length portrait of their president in his academic robes.

Fred Yates was not the only charismatic denizen of the lake country Wilson met that summer. Hardwicke Rawnsley, the Vicar of Crosthwaite Church and Honorary Canon of Carlisle Cathedral, was another. Canon Rawnsley was an extraordinary gifted-man of great versatility – a graduate of Balliol College, Oxford, a world traveller, a prolific writer, poet, lecturer, historian, priest, ardent fell-walker but above all a tireless campaigner for the preservation of the countryside who kept at bay speculative developers and railway companies from despoiling the Lake District. Rawnsley along with Octavia Hill and Robert Hunter formed the National Trust for Places of Historical Interest or Natural Beauty (later shortened to the National Trust). Rawnsley was a friend of Beatrix Potter of *Peter Rabbit* fame who bequeathed to the National Trust her extensive portfolio of Lake District properties. Today the National Trust is the largest landowner in the Lake District National Park with the Potter legacy forming its core holdings.

History does not record the precise date nor the circumstances that brought together the future president of the United States and one of the three founders of the National Trust. According to Mrs Eleanor Rawnsley, Wilson and her husband "had taken some pleasant walks on the fells and had much interesting talk". As Andrew Wilson puts it in his book: "This led to Wilson being invited by Canon Rawnsley to

*Sadly, the journalist, writer and publisher Andrew Wilson died in December 2022.

witness the historic hand-over of Gowbarrow Park, a property on the shores of Ullswater, to the National Trust." The 750 acre Gowbarrow Park (which at the time was in private ownership) consisting of woodland and lush green upland fells including the waterfall Aira Force was the second property bought by public subscription and gifted to the Trust for its protection and benefit of the nation in perpetuity. On August 9, 1906, Woodrow Wilson along with one thousand six hundred enthusiastic supporters of the conservation organisation tramped up the fell overlooking the shores of Ullswater to witness the historic handing-over of the property to the nation for all to enjoy.

For a number of years Woodrow Wilson and Canon Rawnsley remained in touch with each other but their friendship was not quite as devoted nor as close as that between Wilson and the artist Yates.

To the east of Ambleside lies Wansfell Pike, the summit of which provides on clear days unsurpassed views of Windermere, Rydal Water, the Kirkstone Pass and the Troutbeck Valley. As Lakeland fells go Wansfell Pike is of modest height but to gain the summit requires a reasonable level of fitness and agility of foot. The path to the top is uneven and rocky but for those who holiday in the neighbourhood and are reasonably fit it is a rite of passage to climb the fell. While Wilson was picture sitting for Fred Yates, Margaret Wilson along with Mary Yates and a friend climbed to the summit before descending into the Troutbeck Valley on the far side of the fell.

A day or so later Woodrow following in his daughter's footsteps also climbed to the summit of Wansfell Pike before going on to explore the historic village of Troutbeck which straggles the lower southern slopes of the fell. For a reasonably fit walker reaching the summit of Wansfell Pike would not be anything to write home about but for a man recovering from the after effects of a stroke it was quite an achievement as Woodrow later admitted to Ellen, "quite a feat (for me)".

In September, Wilson wrote to a friend in his home country eulogising the Lake District. "No doubt God could have made a lovelier country

Troutbeck Valley – Wilson's "…..wonderland of sweet hills"

A bluebell-lined path wending through the Troutbeck Valley which Woodrow Wilson may have trodden

than this Lake District, but I cannot believe he ever did......I have come to love the region like a second home. We have a little cottage all to ourselves, placed in perhaps the most beautiful spot of all, and our love of the hills and walks has come to be very intimate indeed. I have come to *prefer* rainy weather!" Writing to his philanthropist friend, Cleveland Hoadley Dodge, "I have learned to love Rydal like a second home.....I should like to come to this place of healing every summer, if I could afford the ocean passage so often!"

Wilson interrupted his family holiday in Rydal to see an ophthalmologist in Edinburgh who pronounced his eye "perfectly healed", and a doctor who found his blood pressure only slightly raised. Both clinicians agreed that Wilson could return to work with "proper moderation".

Just as the Wilsons' summer holiday in England was drawing to a close, Woodrow receives a telegram from a newspaper in New Jersey suggesting that his name had been put forward as a candidate for the office of United States senator and "Did he authorize this?" Wilson cabled back from the Post Office in Ambleside."Did not authorize use of my name. Very much complimented that I should be thought of for Senate, but could not leave my work at Princeton."

With his mind turning towards his unfinished work at Princeton, Wilson (and family) boarded the *Caledonia* at Glasgow on October 6. As the ship was steaming down the River Clyde bound for New York, Woodrow wrote an affectionate letter to Fred Yates expressing his and his family's sadness at leaving behind "dear friends".

Two years would pass before Wilson would set foot again in Great Britain. On returning to Princeton he took up the cudgels once more as he fought tooth and nail to persuade his peers, students and alumni to support his democratization program. Once again the physical and emotional effort of trying to push through his program of reforms against stiff opposition took its toll. It would seem that Wilson had only half-heeded the strictures of his Scottish doctors, namely go back to work with "proper moderation". In December 1907, Wilson suffered yet another stroke, albeit a relatively minor one compared with the 1906 episode.

Pondering on her husband's poor health, Ellen decided that he needed a break not only from Princeton but also from her. A cycling holiday in her husband's "beloved Lake District" would, she reckoned, reinvigorate him. At the time Ellen was going through one of her periodic bouts of depression exasperated no doubt by the "Peck" affair (if that is what is was). Their marriage was going through a rocky patch and on the eve of Woodrow's departure for Britain, Ellen made her feelings known about her husband's inappropriate relationship with Mrs Peck. The confrontation between husband and wife must have been distressing for both partners.

With Ellen's rebuke still ringing in his ears, Wilson boarded the *California* in June 1908. As the ship steamed down the Hudson River and out into the Atlantic bound for Glasgow a contrite husband took pen to paper to write to his wife. "It will probably be the twelfth of July before I am on the road and headed for the Lakes, but I shall try to find some means of diversion, and every day my love for my darling will be my chief joy, my chief disturbance!"

Throughout his summer vacation in England, Wilson wrote a stream of highly affectionate letters to Ellen (or Eileen as he sometimes called her using her Irish name) in which he avowed his love for her. As Andrew Wilson puts it in his book: "His letters to his wife during this visit are the most descriptive and lyrical that he ever wrote to her." Wordsworthian in every sense although the great romantic poet was no angel himself having an illegitimate daughter following an affair with Annette Vallon during his walking tour of France in 1790.

The *California* docked at midnight on 28 June and by morning Wilson had booked into the Grand Hotel in Glasgow. After a night or two at the Grand, Wilson travelled by train across central Scotland to its former capital Sterling. From Sterling he travelled by train to Edinburgh and then caught another to Lockerbie where he took to his "wheels" in very wet conditions. His bicycle had no mudguards over the wheels....."and all the wetness of the road was thrown up on me and on the bicycle at every revolution". He was wearing a blue shirt and knee-length shorts, a long waterproof cape, an ancient golf cap with a peaked visor..... and, according to the memoirs of Stockton Axson, "His pockets bulged with few necessities – a toothbrush, a comb, a change of underwear and the Oxford Book of English Verse."

From the border town of Lockerbie, Wilson cycled to Carlisle where after a twelve-year hiatus he resumed his search for his mother's place of birth. On or about July 12 he wrote to Ellen: "I have at last found the locality of the house, under the castle walls in which dear mother was born." Mission accomplished, Wilson had time on his hands to visit Carlisle's medieval cathedral.

From Carlisle the college president cycled to Keswick via Penrith. By now this area of north-west England must have been familiar territory. In a letter to Ellen, Woodrow acknowledged that his muscles "rather soft for the business of steady wheeling". That summer northern England and southern Scotland were having a prolonged spell of near record-breaking high temperatures which no doubt would have added to Wilson's discomfort. The cycling mad professor was now in his fifty-second year, so perhaps it is hardly surprising that his muscles ached after so much wheeling. After a two-day stopover in Keswick, Wilson mounted his "silent steed" and retraced the route through the Thirlmere Valley made in the summer of 1896, arriving in Grasmere at midday on July 15.

Before his departure for his summer vacation in the Lake District, Fred Yates had written to Wilson suggesting that for the duration of his forthcoming visit he should rent a small cottage as he had done when he came over with Ellen and the children. However, Wilson eschewed this idea by booking a small room at the Rothay Hotel in Grasmere. After lunching at the hotel, Wilson lost no time in walking over to Rydal for a reunion with his artist friend. Wilson took the picturesque path which runs below the southern flank of Nab Scar. Since Wilson's last visit, Fred and his family had relocated to Hart Head Cottage, a newly built property situated higher up the hillside overlooking the rooftops of Rydal and its sheet of water.

In a letter to Ellen he wrote: "Ah, my dear, my dear, what a walk it was! Every foot of it was eloquent of you – and all my dear ones. At every turn I came upon some tree or nook or sweet outlook that you had admired and loved.....and then I found Yates!....I knocked at the door, Mrs Yates opened it, and we faced one another with delight. She almost embraced me. Yates himself was in the garden up the hillside, putting in some lettuce, and, before my greetings with Mrs Yates were over, I had him, too, by the hand."

Once he had settled into his hotel (which was to be his base for the next ten weeks), Wilson ventured out on to the fells. He informed Ellen in a letter written on July 30 that he was much fitter and stronger than when he had first arrived in England and to underscore the point he had the previous day walked over to the Kirkstone Pass and returned to his hotel via the Troutbeck Valley calling in at *The Mortal Man Inn* for lunch. The intriguingly named inn stands in a commanding position at the head of Troutbeck with its medley of 17th-and 18th-century buildings grouped around three wells dedicated to various saints. At the lower end of the settlement stands a 17th-century *Statesman* farmhouse with cylindrical chimneys in the vernacular-style of architecture redolent of Westmorland. On his previous visit to Troutbeck, Wilson had expressed an interest in buying the old farmstead which at the time was owned by a local family (the National Trust acquired the property in 1948).

Writing to a Princeton colleague, Wilson proclaimed: "I am having a very restful and enjoyable time. This [hotel] is my headquarters. I make frequent sallies into different parts of the District, either afoot or on my wheel, and I am sufficiently acquainted hereabouts to have a very pleasant, and sufficiently large circle of friends, who keep my mind and

The Wordsworth Hotel, Grasmere (formerly the Rothay Hotel), a firm favourite with Woodrow Wilson

Townend, Troutbeck 1668 (circa) - Wilson expressed an interest in buying the farmstead

heart, from affairs Princetonian."

This being Wilson's fifth visit to the English lakes, he was by now pretty well acquainted with the valleys of Ullswater, Troutbeck and Thirlmere, the vale of Grasmere, the towns of Windermere, Ambleside and Keswick and their satellite villages and hamlets, not to mention the lakes in the northern and central regions of the Lake District. One area he had not so far explored was the far western valleys and lakes which lie close to the Irish Sea.

On July 20th, Wilson once again took to the road with his bicycle heading this time for the far western region of Lakeland. From Grasmere he cycled over "hills, hills, hills, nothing but hills" to Coniston railway station where he boarded a train for Broughton-in-Furness. (Today this rail journey would not be possible as the Coniston line was closed in 1962 – yet another scenic branch line that British Railways axed on the recommendation of its chairman, Dr Beeching.)

From Broughton, Wilson explored the *timeless* Duddon Valley (whether he cycled the entire length of the rugged valley – unlikely – or merely concentrated on its lower reaches, he does not say). The narrow valley is drained by one of the most delightful watercourses in Lakeland, the River Duddon which rises amongst the high fells of central Lakeland where two thousand years ago the Romans built a high-level road and a fort at *Mediobocdum*. The river flows south-west eventually losing its identity as its fresh waters meet the salt-water channels of the Duddon Estuary.

The valley has changed little since Wordsworth penned:

> *Time, in most cases, and nature everywhere have given a*
> *sanctity to the humble works of man, that are scattered*
> *over peaceful retirement.*

(Notes to The River Duddon, a Series of Sonnets, 1820).

Lake District Summers

Wilson regretted that he had not read the *Duddon Sonnets* prior to his visit but he was pleased that he "saw the whole valley with fresh eyes".

The professor stayed the night at Broughton, possibly in one of the inns overlooking the Georgian market square. The next day he took a train for Drigg, a coastal village not far from the 2nd-century Roman port of Ravenglass. From Drigg he cycled inland towards Wasdale "mile after mile of delicious shaded lanes" that lead unerringly to England's deepest and most mysterious lake, Wastwater. An excitable Wilson wrote to Ellen "sheer skrees [sic] that descend precipitously from a great height into the southern side of the unfathomable lake". Wilson was impressed, as indeed are most first time visitors, by the starkness of the landscape and the great wall of near vertical, loose screes that fall away into the deep waters of the glacial lake.

At the northern head of Wastwater lies a great amphitheatre of volcanic fells – Great Gable, Pillar, Sca Fell and the highest mountain in England, Scafell Pike. Having resisted the urge to climb Scafell Pike – de rigueur for those with a passion for high-level fell walking – Wilson later wrote to Ellen "loved it all and lingered, in a sort of fascination". The experience had exceeded his expectations.

The following day the future president of the United States headed north along the coast to explore the remotest and least accessible of the Lake District dales – Ennerdale with its eponymous lake. Wilson informed his brother-in-law, Stockton, that Ennerdale had "the quiet remote beauty of a nun".

Wilson was fortunate to see Ennerdale before the head of the dale was disfigured by the planting of regimented waves of dull conifer trees. (However, this blot on the landscape did not deter another future president of the United States – sixty-three years after Wilson's visit – from proposing marriage to one Miss Hilary Rodham above the banks of Ennerdale Water. Whether Bill Clinton had in mind "the quiet..... beauty of a nun" when he got down on his knee is not known.)

Ennerdale Water

Duddon Valley

Lake District Summers

From romantic Ennerdale, Wilson rode through the western dales to Cockermouth where he caught a train for Keswick before boarding a coach to take him and his bicycle back to his base in Grasmere.

On August 10, Wilson interrupted his summer vacation at Grasmere to visit Andrew Carnegie, the Scottish-American industrialist, at his seat at Skibo Castle in Scotland. The two men were already acquainted. Wilson, trading on his Scottish heritage, had some years earlier persuaded the steel baron to open his cheque book. The philanthropist duly obliged by donating a large sum of money to Princeton to build a lake so its students could compete with Harvard, Yale and Columbia at rowing! The rowing lake was not quite what Wilson had in mind but the great philanthropist insisted on a rowing lake. Apparently Carnegie disapproved of football and "that rowing would take the young men's minds off football".

In a letter to Ellen, Wilson likened Skibo Castle to a luxurious hotel where up to twenty-five people would sit down for every meal. "There was everything to do that you can think of: hunting, fishing, golfing, sailing, swimming in the most beautiful swimming pool I ever saw..., driving, motoring, billiards, tennis, croquet; and there was perfect freedom to do as you pleased..... The estate is some twenty miles long and...about six miles broad." Despite the multifarious activities available to the guests, Wilson was "eager to get back to the little Rothay Hotel and the more simple friends at the dear Lakes. I am tired and in a humour to be entirely my own master again...."

Wilson arrived back in Grasmere on August 17. Time was rapidly running out. His steamship the *Caledonia* taking him back to New York was due to sail from Glasgow on Saturday, September 5. For the next two weeks Wilson's diary was filled with social engagements with the great and good of Grasmere and neighbourhood. On August 21, Wilson attended the sheep dog trials in the Troutbeck Valley. "It was one of the most glorious days I have ever seen in this wonderland of sweet hills and the magic of sun and shadow." He paid frequent visits to Hart Head Cottage for sittings with Fred Yates who was putting the finishing touches to a portrait of Wilson which he had started painting shortly after his friend had arrived in Grasmere.

After "saying goodbye to the kind people who have made his summer so pleasant.....", Wilson with his bicycle crated for transit and Fred's painting safely stored amongst his luggage left Grasmere on Wednesday, September 2, 1908. Wilson would never again return to his "beloved Lake District". His life was about to be consumed by politics and public service which when set against his academic posts afforded fewer opportunities to take extended vacations overseas. Also the international situation was deteriorating. Britain and Germany were engaged in an arms race. Germany under the direction of Kaiser Wilhelm II and his Prussian commanders was rapidly building up her navy. Neither nation seemed capable of finding the wherewithal to reverse the steady drift towards war.

On returning to Princeton, Wilson continued to campaign for the adoption of his reform program but largely to no avail. In September 1910, Wilson wrote to Fred Yates: "It seems probable that I shall be nominated for the office of Governorship of New Jersey by the Democrats of the State at their convention on next Thursday, the 15th, and I must take it if it comes." Which of course he did, and in so doing was taking the first step on the road to becoming the 28th president of the United States.

Governor Wilson and Ellen and their three daughters

Chapter Six

Honours Bestowed

"I don't know whether war is an interlude during peace, or peace is an interlude during war." Georges Clemenceau.

In the closing stages of the Great War, Woodrow Wilson delivered a speech to Congress outlining what he considered to be the root causes of the conflict and enunciated fourteen points as the basis for bringing about an enduring peace after the guns fall silent. The speech is known as the Fourteen Points and in the final days of the war was accepted by the German Government as the basis for the terms of surrender. The Armistice signed by Germany and the Allies ended military operations on land and at sea but did not end the war itself. To bring the war to a formal end required a peace treaty signed between Germany, the Allied powers and the United States. Paris was chosen as the place to hold the Peace Conference although the decision was not welcomed by the British Prime Minister David Lloyd George who only relented after tearful pleadings by the seventy-seven year old French Premier Georges Clemenceau.

After taking soundings Woodrow Wilson decided that he would personally attend the Paris Peace Conference although not everyone in Washington was in favour of him going over. Robert Lansing, Wilson's secretary of state, counselled against going to Paris. "I told him frankly that I thought the plan to attend was unwise and would be a mistake....." Lansing thought that Wilson could "practically dictate the terms of peace if he held aloof". The president was having none of it – he wanted to be in the thick of the action, not on the sidelines 4000 miles away in Washington. Historians have since questioned the wisdom of Wilson's decision to head the United States' delegation in Paris.

The American entourage headed by the president boarded the troopship *George Washington* on December 4, 1918. After an uneventful passage the ocean liner docked at the Brittany port of Brest on December 13. The president with his wife by his side were taken by open car through the streets of Brest where they were greeted by ecstatic crowds, many dressed in traditional Breton costumes throwing flowers and shouting *"Vive l'Amérique! Vive Wilson!"* The air vibrated with the skirl of bagpipes. A victorious emperor returning to ancient Rome after a successful military campaign in a foreign land could not have received a more enthusiastic welcome than that accorded by the Bretons to the American president and first lady.

The scenes in Brest were repeated in Paris the next day. The president, his daughter Margaret (who had come over to France to greet her father), the first lady, the president of France Raymond Poincaré and his wife rode down the Champs-Élysées in open horse-drawn carriages escorted by the mounted Garde Républicaine. As a mark of honour the procession passed under the world famous Arc de Triomphe.

Presidents Wilson and Poincare head a jubilant procession of open horse-drawn carriages to wild cheering from Parisians

Honours Bestowed

Thousands upon thousands of Parisians lining the sidewalks and hanging out of windows cheered wildly as the procession passed by.

President Wilson, the first lady and her social secretary and Dr Cary Grayson had been assigned the Palace Murat as their living quarters for the duration of the peace conference. Colonel Edward House and the rest of the American delegation including Robert Lansing, Henry White and General Tasker Howard Bliss were housed in considerable luxury at the Hôtel de Crillon, located some distance away from the Palace Murat.

Wilson was hoping that the peace conference would get underway shortly after his arrival in Paris but there seemed a marked reluctance on the part of Britain, France and Italy to begin the negotiations straightaway. There arose a number of logistical problems that had to be resolved before the representatives could get down to business. This allowed Wilson to honour pledges he had made to visit the capital cities of the Allied powers.

Christmas Day was spent with General "Black Jack" Pershing and his troops and on Boxing Day the Wilsons together with a large contingent of staff, journalists and cinematograph operators boarded a train for Calais. From the French port the presidential party crossed the English Channel in the hospital ship *Brighton* escorted by seven destroyers festooned in flags with the stars and stripes being flown from the masthead of every vessel. The short sea crossing to Dover was made under a gentle swell and a blue sky. A twenty-one gun salute fired from one of the vessels in the flotilla welcomed the president and his party to England. As the party disembarked, a squadron of RAF planes flew overhead in formation. Woodrow Wilson was the first incumbent president of the United States to visit Great Britain. To the strains of the *Star Spangled Banner*, the president inspected the guards of honour. After formal introductions to a coterie of dignitaries assembled on the pier and a welcoming address read by the recorder on behalf of the aldermen and burgesses of the Borough of Dover, the presidential party boarded a special train for London.

Honours Bestowed

The presidential party was met at Charing Cross Station by King George V and Queen Mary. A cavalcade headed by horse-drawn open carriages set off from the station for Buckingham Palace via Trafalgar Square. Along the two-mile route two million Londoners – according to one well-placed source – turned out to see the procession. "...roofs, windows, trees and posts were laden with humanity", recalled Edith Wilson in her memoirs. Guns boomed out in salute. Everywhere flags – the union jack and the stars and stripes – fluttered in the late December sunshine. Twenty thousand soldiers with bayonets lined the route. Guards in khaki uniform rode ahead of the royal carriages. The crowds roared and cheered as they caught sight of the first carriage with the American president sitting alongside the king. In response to the rapturous reception, Wilson raised his tall hat made of silk and gave the broadest of smiles. Maybe he was thinking how proud his English-born mother would have been to see the welcome London is giving to her first-born son. The nation's capital had seen nothing like it since the Coronation of George V and Mary on June 22, 1911. Aeroplanes in arrowhead formation flew overhead. Huge crowds had assembled in the Mall and around the Victoria Monument opposite Buckingham Palace in anticipation of a balcony appearance by the two heads of state and their wives. They were not disappointed. Not long after the cavalcade swept into the grounds of the palace, King George V and Queen Mary and their only daughter Princess Mary stepped-out onto the famous balcony followed by Mr and Mrs Wilson. The president made a short address to the enthusiastic crowds milling below the balcony but the speech was drowned out by the exuberant cheering.

Later that evening the Wilsons attended a state banquet hosted by King George V. The president and first lady stayed two nights at the palace. It is interesting to speculate whether the former president of Princeton contrasted his sumptuous suite at the palace with the modest hotel room in Grasmere where a decade earlier he had spent the summer with his Lake District friends.

Two heads of State Woodrow Wilson and King George V. The photograph was taken outside Buckingham Palace on the president's birthday in 1918

The president and first lady arriving at the Mansion House, London – December, 28, 1918

Honours Bestowed

"A pilgrimage of the heart." Woodrow Wilson on visiting Carlisle, the birth-place of his mother.

On December 27, 1918, Woodrow Wilson lunched with Britain's prime minster, David Lloyd George – their first face to face encounter – at No 10 Downing Street. Wilson also for the first time met Winston Churchill and other members of the administration. In the evening the Wilsons dined with George V and Queen Mary. The following day (Saturday) Wilson celebrated his sixty-second birthday. King George V came to the guest suite with a gift of books on the history of Windsor Castle and to congratulate the president. Later that day Woodrow and Edith went by horse-drawn open carriage to the medieval Guildhall Hall in the City of London where the president was granted Freedom of the City.

At midnight the presidential party boarded the royal train that was to take them to Carlisle."A pilgrimage of the heart" in the words of Wilson. Just before nine-thirty on Sunday morning the royal train drew up alongside the platform at Carlisle's Citadel. The rain was pouring down in torrents. Edith later recalled: "As I looked from the window of my stateroom I had the impression of entering a forest of giant toadstools. All I could see was a mass of dripping umbrellas manoeuvring for places nearer the train. The whole population had turned out and a sturdy-looking lot they were." A great deal of water had flowed under the bridge since Wilson's last visit to Carlisle where he finally succeeded in locating the place (but not the actual house which had been demolished) where his mother was born.

After stepping out of the royal train the president and his wife were received by the mayor and mayoress and the city burgesses. A reception for the presidential party had been arranged at the Crown & Mitre Hotel, a hotel not unfamiliar to Wilson who first stayed there in July 1906. The route from the railway station to the hotel was lined by local residents who despite the torrential rain had turned out to greet the president and his wife with hearty cheers. At the hotel the town clerk presented to the president a stream of local people who through letters, documents, memoranda and newspaper cuttings linked the president's grandfather, Reverend Thomas Woodrow, with Carlisle. Also present at the reception was Canon Rawnsley and his wife. The canon's presence may have stirred in Wilson memories of the day he tramped up Gowbarrow Fell above Ullswater at the dawn of the National Trust. Before departing the hotel, Wilson had the honour of being granted Freeman of the City.

From the hotel the president was driven around varies sites in Carlisle associated with his mother and grandfather. The highlight of the visit was a Sunday church service held at Lowther Street Congregational Church which began with the singing of *Mine Eyes Have Seen the Glory*. During the service the pastor invited the president to address the congregation. Edith Wilson later recorded: "This was totally unexpected, and when my husband rose, I wondered what he would say. Certainly I have never heard him speak more eloquently or straight from his heart. There was not a sound except his voice accompanied by the steady, gentle patter of rain on the roof. As he stood there, I thought of that little girl, his mother....and how proud she would have been of him. Someway her spirit seemed very near him there, and the tribute he paid to her was to a real and gracious presence."

After the church service Woodrow and Edith were taken by car to the cathedral where they were received by the bishop, the dean and Canon Rawnsley. The visitors were taken around the cathedral and shown the chapel where the novelist Sir Walter Scott was married and the spot where Robert Bruce signed his allegiance to the English Crown. As the guests were leaving the cathedral, Canon Rawnsley turning to the president said: "The next time we see you we hope it will be in the Lake Country." The president replied: "I hope so." Canon Rawnsley was the only representative at the reception of Wilson's Lake District friends. Fred Yates, the closest friend of all, was too poorly to attend and remained at home in Rydal.

When all the prearranged engagements were completed in Carlisle the

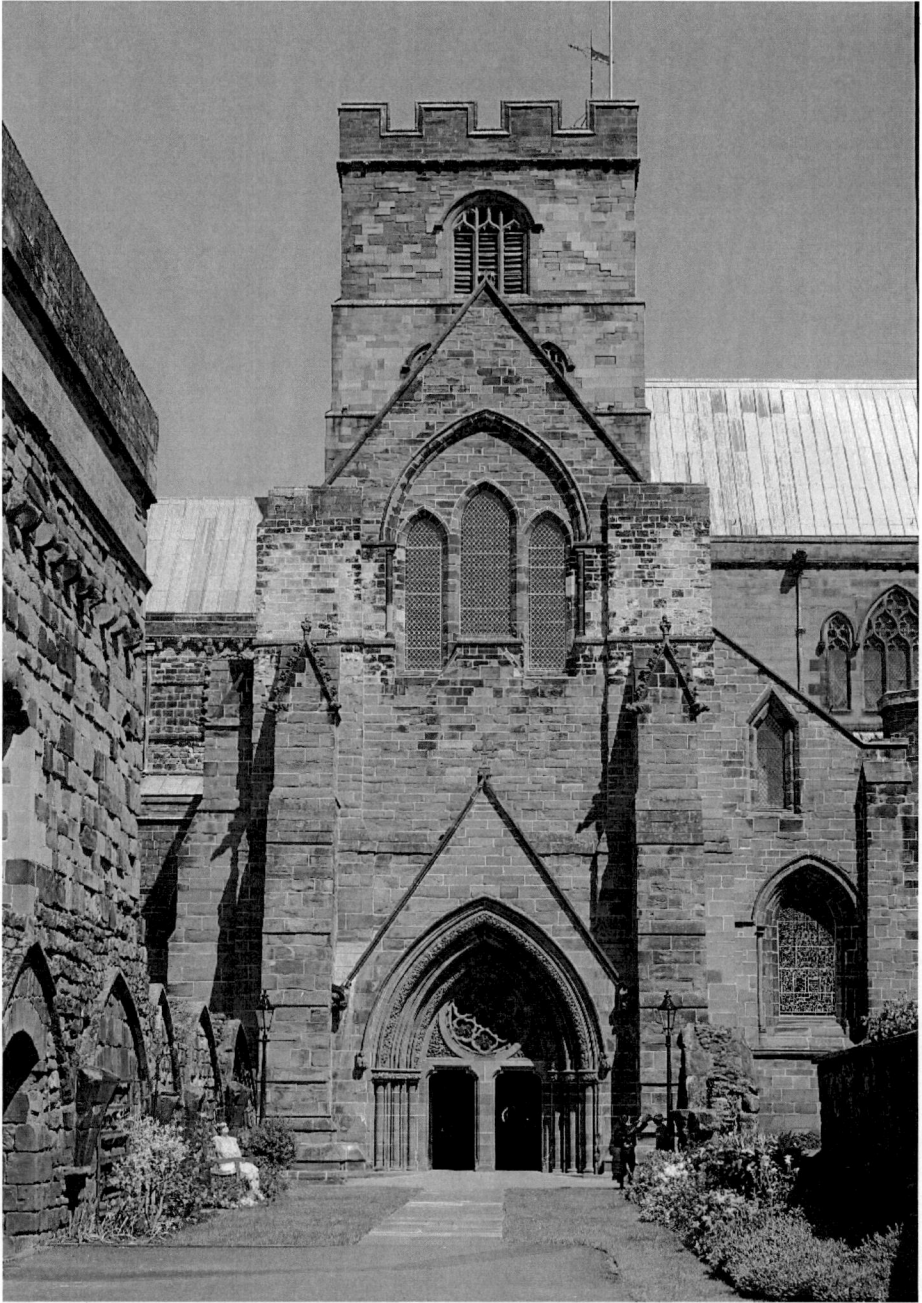

Carlisle Cathedral founded by the Normans and largely completed by the end of the 14th-century

presidential party boarded the royal train that was to take them to Manchester where at the Free Trade Hall the Freedom of the City was bestowed on the president in recognition of his services in bringing an end to the war.

From Manchester the presidential party returned to London. In the evening of December 30, 1918, King George V and Queen Mary gave a farewell dinner for the president and his wife. On New Year's Eve the Wilsons left London for France and the Peace Conference. Woodrow Wilson would never again set foot on British soil.

It was finally settled that the Peace Conference would open on January 18, 1919. This allowed the Wilsons to continue their jubilatory tour of Europe. After a brief stopover in Paris, the Wilsons travelled to Rome by train where they were greeted by King Victor Emnanuel III and members of the Italian Government. The presidential party joined Queen Elena in a cavalcade of horse-drawn open carriages escorted by mounted soldiers in ceremonial dress uniforms through the historic streets and piazzas to the Quirinal Palace. As in Paris and London the reception the presidential party received from the public who had turned out in their hundreds of thousands was overwhelming.

The following day the president and first lady together with Dr Grayson had an audience with Pope Benedict XV at the Vatican. The audience was highly significant for two reasons. At the time there was a great deal of hostility amongst the Protestant community in America towards the recent waves of Catholic immigrants. Secondly, Wilson was the first president of the United States to be granted an audience with the pope.

From Rome the presidential party moved on to Milan where a visit to the world-famous opera house, La Scala, is almost obligatory. Edith Wilson was disappointed with the opera house which she thought was "plain" in comparison with the opera houses in Paris, Vienna and Berlin. The presidential party was treated to a performance of Verdi's *Aida*. The Wilsons, though far from opera buffs, seemed to have enjoyed the opera although they were promised a more "sacred concert". Edith later recalled that it was "a magnificent spectacle and I have always been glad they did it. Secretly, I think my husband was too....." From Milan, the party went on to Turin where the president was awarded an honorary degree from the University of Turin. While in Turin, Wilson received news that his old adversary, former President Roosevelt, had died.

Chapter Seven

Down to Business

"I wish in my soul the President had appointed me as Chairman of the Peace Delegation....." Colonel Edward House.

On January 7, 1919, the Wilsons arrived back in Paris. The Peace Conference was formally opened on January 18, 1919 at the Quai d'Orsay under the chairmanship of Georges Clemenceau. The objective of the conference was to establish the terms of peace following the signing of the Armistice agreement with Germany. Thirty or so nations participated in the conference but the proceedings were dominated by the United States, Great Britain, France and Italy (the "Big Four" as they became known) and to a lesser extent Japan which initially was one of the major participants but later took a back seat as the country had little interest in European affairs.

From left to right: David Lloyd George, Vittorio Orlando, Georges Clemenceau and Woodrow Wilson at the Paris Peace Conference

Down to Business

From the outset the conference was beset by problems. The absence of important nations undermined the peace talks. Russia was not invited because the new Bolshevik Government had defaulted on repaying its outstanding financial debts to the Allied powers and the United States. The defeated nations including Germany, Austria, Hungary, Bulgaria and Turkey were excluded from the discussions. Pre-existing treaties entered into by the Allied nations created another major impediment, whereas the United States was entering into the peace talks with a clean slate. The Big Four controlled the conference but from the beginning were at loggerheads over the agenda. Wilson was pushing hard for the planned formation of the League of Nations (his main goal) and the concept that all nations should have the right to "self determination". Wilson insisted that the League of Nations should take precedence over all other issues. On the other hand, France, Britain and Italy were primarily interested in the redistribution of territories colonised by Germany, financial reparations and the disarmament of Germany, especially its navy which for Great Britain was a *sine qua non*.

The negotiations were glacially slow and tortuous. Woodrow Wilson led the main discussions and chaired the meetings working closely with British Prime Minister David Lloyd George, French Premier Georges Clemenceau and Italian Premier Vittorio Orlando. Wilson was actively involved in the drafting and redrafting of the peace treaty based on his Fourteen Points of which Clemenceau was dismissive. "Mr Wilson bores me with his Fourteen Points. Why, God Almighty has only ten!" With single-mindedness to the point of obstinacy, Wilson pursued his overriding objective – the League of Nations. The years he had spent at Princeton persuading, cajoling and arguing with his colleagues to accept his reform program were now reaping dividends as the other premiers reluctantly gave way to Wilson over the League of Nations.

Matters were not helped by Wilson's initial dislike of Clemenceau (who had lived for a period in New York, spoke fluent English and was for a time married to a woman from New England) whom he found duplicitous. "The French people are the hardest I ever tried to do business with," complained Wilson. David Lloyd George summed up Clemenceau in a single sentence. "He loved France but hated all Frenchmen." Nor was Clemenceau over-keen on either Wilson or Lloyd George. The British prime minister, the youngest of the foursome, he found devious and untrustworthy, intuitive rather than intellectual. As for Wilson, "I do not think he is a bad man, but I have not yet made up my mind as to how much of him is good.....I find myself between Jesus Christ on the one hand and Napoléon Bonaparte on the other," he quipped. Notwithstanding their profound differences over the terms of the peace settlement, Wilson's personal relationships with Lloyd George, Clemenceau and Orlando were according to Grayson "generally pleasant and cordial" and "his daily conferences with the three premiers were patient and oftentimes humorous."

Lloyd George, unlike Wilson and Clemenceau, was not a politician to bear ill will towards his opponents. He was generally good-natured. The British prime minister was married with five children, one of whom had died aged seventeen. Over the years he and his wife had grown apart. He had a reputation for being something of a ladies' man and was no stranger to extra-marital relationships which at times had brought him close to political disaster. By 1919, he had settled down with a single mistress, Frances Stevenson, a young intelligent woman who ran his office and was by his side in Paris. Late in life following the death of his wife, Lloyd George and Frances Stevenson married.

As tensions mounted amongst the Big Four even Wilson's loyal servant Colonel Edward House was briefing against his boss. Perhaps this was sour grapes on the part of House who thought that he should have led the American negotiating team in Paris. House confided in his diary: "I wish in my soul the President had appointed me as Chairman of the Peace Delegation...."

By mid-February, despite all the differences between the Big Four, sufficient progress had been made on the League of Nations project for

Down to Business

Wilson to take leave, at least temporarily, and return to the United States leaving the honorary colonel holding the fort. By way of reassurance House informed Wilson that he "could button everything up in the next four weeks.....and to bear in mind while he was gone that it is sometimes necessary to compromise in order to get things done"

The Wilsons accompanied by Dr Grayson and the president's press secretary, Ray Stannard Baker, boarded the *George Washington* which sailed on February 15, 1919 arriving in Boston (a strike by longshoremen prevented the vessel from docking in New York) eight days later.

Wilson's homecoming was rather low-key in comparison with the rapturous reception he had received in Europe. After dealing with pressing domestic issues, Wilson turned his attention to garnering support for the League of Nations. Congressmen on the Democratic side of the aisle were generally pro-League but Republicans on the other side were sceptical about its inclusion in the peace treaty. The Senate was bitterly divided on the issue. If the treaty was to bind the United States not less than two-thirds of the membership of the upper house would have to vote for its ratification. Those who opposed the League argued that it violated the Monroe doctrine which, although couched in diplomatic language, was a message to Europe from President Monroe to keep out of our backyard which he defined as North and South America. In return the United States would not interfere in the internal affairs of Europe. At the time, the Monroe doctrine had never been accepted by the European nations or, indeed, by Japan which in 1912 came within its sphere. It was a unilateral declaration made by an American president at a time when the Spanish colonies in South America were gaining their independence and there was a fear that Spain or another European power would try to recolonise them. The doctrine had no legal standing outside the United States and even within the States it has been denounced. Wilson was now paying the price for not including senior Republican senators in the American delegation. Despite failing to win over Republican senators, the president was in a defiant mood – not in the least receptive to making compromises over the League to accommodate the concerns of those who opposed ratification. Wilson's intransigence would eventually take him down a path that would not only have far-reaching consequences for his administration but would bring to a premature end his political career.

Before departing for Paris to resume the peace talks, the president found time to write to his English friend, Fred Yates, who was in a London clinic awaiting a major operation. Fred in a letter to the president regretted that illness had prevented him from seeing him when he visited Carlisle and Manchester. "My house is in order, bills all paid, my will made and Mary taking on the duties should anything occur.....I know you love us, Your friend, FRED YATES."

The artist, sadly, did not survive the operation; he died on February 11 aged sixty-four. Not knowing that his friend had died, Wilson replied on February 26. "My dear Fred: Your letter gave me a pang, because it spoke of an immediate operation, but its date, the fourth of February, encourages me to believe that by this time you have not only come through but are beginning to feel a bit normal again. My heart goes out to you. It was generous of you to write to me, and you may be sure that it touched me very much. I want you to know how deeply you have established yourself in my admiration and affection. Please give my love to the dear ones, and above all things take care of yourself and get strong." Wilson learnt of his friend's death on March 2 when Canon Rawnsley cabled to say that Fred had died following his operation.

The Wilsons, Dr Cary Grayson and Ray Stannard Baker returned to France on board the *George Washington* which docked in Brest on March 13, 1919. The presidential party was assigned a new residence at 11 place des États-Unis. Their new accommodation was less prestigious than the Palace Murat but being opposite the temporary residence of Lloyd George allowed the two leaders to meet frequently. (In the public mind it is often thought, mistakenly, that the historic Palace of

This photograph is of painting by the Irish artist Sir William Orpen depicting Woodrow Wilson flanked by the prime ministers of France, Italy and Great Britain. Wilson's chair is higher than the other members of the Council reflecting his senior status as head of state as well as chief executive. The peacemakers are positioned in front of the magnificent marble fireplace inside the Quai d'Orsay, Paris. Credit: Imperial War Museum.

Down to Business

Versailles was the venue for the Peace Conference. The actual signing of the treaty took place in the great palace built by Louis XIV, whereas most of the negotiations on the peace settlement took place either in Wilson's private study or the Quai d'Orsay in central Paris.)

During Wilson's absence, Colonel House had reached a preliminary agreement on difficult issues including boundaries, colonies and reparations. In a debriefing session with Wilson, the colonel reiterated what he had told the president before leaving Paris, namely that in order to reach a preliminary agreement he had had to make certain compromises. Edith Wilson later recorded that her husband's meeting with House had put ten years on his age. "House has given away everything I had won before we left Paris.". Whether Edith's recollection of her husband's reaction to the debriefing is entirely accurate is open to question given that Edith had an axe to grind. She disliked House; her animosity towards him seems to have stemmed from the time the colonel cautioned Wilson against marrying Edith so soon after the death of Ellen. But what is not in doubt, the relationship between Wilson and House was never the same after the debriefing. Woodrow and Edith had a strong bond of loyalty to each other when it came to casting aside colleagues and associates. If one spouse disliked someone the other spouse would invariably follow suit.

Edward House had boasted to the president that in his absence he could "button everything up in the next four weeks". His statement turned out to be wildly optimistic for it took another four months of interminable arguments, stand-offs, walk-outs and political wrangling before the terms of the main treaty were finally settled between the Council of Four. By this time Orlando (whose grasp of English was rudimentary) had taken his bat and ball home and rarely attended the talks unless it was to discuss Italy's claims in the Adriatic.

The strain of it all was undermining Wilson's fragile health. On April 3, Wilson fell ill. He reported intense pains in his back, stomach and head. He was running a fever and coughing violently. At the time the Spanish flu (which had killed and was still killing millions around the world) was in its second year, and Wilson had so far dodged the bullet. Whether the president had finally succumbed to the pandemic is questionable but it would seem that he had gone down with a virus of sorts (although Lloyd George speculated that Wilson had suffered a stroke) that confined him to his bedroom for several days. As May came around the overworked and fatigued president began to suffer memory lapses and at times his speech was incoherent, often he could not recall the day's discussions. Frequently he would lose control of his temper.

By June the Big Four were in a position to present to the German Government the final terms of the peace settlement although there was a last minute hiccup when Lloyd George sought to water-down the clauses dealing with reparations, borders and the Rhineland which the British cabinet considered were too harsh on Germany. Wilson stood his ground and rejected this last minute intervention.

While the German Government was considering the peace treaty, the Wilsons accompanied by Herbert Hoover left Paris for a two-day state visit to Belgium. They were met by King Albert I and his queen who accompanied the presidential party on an emotional motor-tour through the battlefields of Flanders and Ypres. The latter had become synonymous with trench warfare; its terrain had hosted some of the bloodiest battles ever fought by mankind. Once again the Wilsons were greeted by huge enthusiastic crowds lining the streets as the motor convoy passed through the bombed-out villages and towns.

On the second day of the state visit, Wilson addressed the Belgium state parliament where he underlined the importance of the League. "The League of Nations is the child of this great war for right....." Then taking aim at the dissident senators back home in Washington DC he declared: "Any nation which declines to adhere to this Covenant deliberately turns away from the most telling appeal that has ever been made to its conscience and its manhood." The word "Covenant" with its Scottish 17th-century Presbyterian roots would perhaps today be replaced with the word "Article".

Down to Business

The presidential party returned to Paris half-expecting the German Government to reject the peace terms; however a mere two hours before the deadline for acceptance a reconstituted German Government signalled its intention to sign the peace treaty.

It is outside the scope of this work to expatiate on an immensely complex treaty – a treaty which together with a series of treaties emanating from the peace conference would redraw the world map. In a nutshell, the Council of Four agreed that Alsace-Lorraine would be returned to France. Poland would be reconstituted as an independent country with Germany, Austria-Hungary and Russia ceding territory to the new nation. (It was Colonel Edward House, rather than Wilson, who pressed strongly for an independent Poland. Had it not been for House, Poland may well have been folded into Russia.) Denmark would

The medieval Cloth Hall, and Cathedral at Ypres lie in ruins following heavy repeated shelling and artillery fire. Artist: James Kerr Lawson. Credit: Canadian War Museum.

acquire northern Schlewig. German borders would be redrawn to provide Belgium and Lithuania with more land. In total Germany would loose thirteen per cent of its pre-war land mass (approximately 27,000 square miles) and between six and seven million of its people. Clemenceau wanted to go much further and dismantle Germany completely but Wilson and Lloyd George strongly resisted his demands causing simmering resentment in the old man. It was agreed that the German state of Rhineland would be demilitarized and that Germany's military would be restricted to one hundred and fifteen thousand men. After much fractious argument it was settled that Germany would be stripped of its overseas colonies in Africa, the Pacific and China. Germany would be required to pay substantial reparations to cover civilian damage caused by its military actions. Reparations were a highly contentious issue. John Maynard Keynes, who was present during the negotiations in Paris, called the treaty a Carthaginian peace that would economically destroy Germany.

The treaty left the position of the kaiser who had fled to the Netherlands, a country friendly to Germany, in a state of limbo. The treaty called for him to be tried for war crimes before a special tribunal of five judges drawn one each from the Great Powers. However, he could only face trial if an application for extradition was successful. In the event the Netherlands refused to extradite him. The refusal could not be enforced through the League of Nations as the Netherlands never sought membership of the League. From his safe-home in the Netherlands the kaiser lived long enough to see the rise of Hitler whom he cheered as Germany resumed arm hostilities in the late 1930s.

The humiliation of surrendering was too much to bear for a number of high ranking German military personnel. The treaty (at the insistence of Lloyd George) called for the surrender of the German battle-fleet. Its unrepentant commander committed suicide but not before issuing an order for the battle-fleet to be scuppered at Scapa Flow off the coast of Scotland.

Down to Business

It was agreed that the signing ceremony would take place in the magnificent Hall of Mirrors inside the palace at Versailles. The venue for the signing ceremony was of huge symbolic significance for the French nation. The Hall of Mirrors was where on February 26, 1871 the preliminary peace treaty between Germany and France was signed following France's defeat in its war with Prussia. Six weeks earlier the Hall of Mirrors was the surprising venue where Bismarck proclaimed the German Empire by uniting the kingdoms of Prussia, Bavaria, Saxony and Wurttemberg. It was in the Hall of Mirrors that Kaiser Wilhelm I – former king of Prussia and grandfather of Kaiser Wilhelm II – was elected head of state of the new nation.

In bright sunshine on June 28, 1919 delegates, spectators, reporters, secretaries, cinematograph operators, photographers and artists commissioned to paint the signing ceremony arrived at the Palace of Versailles. Just before two-o'clock in the afternoon they all filed into the Hall of Mirrors. One hour later two representatives – Hermann Müller and Johannes Bell – of the new German Government came forward under escort and sat at the Louis XIV table (the very table where in 1871 humiliated France signed the preliminary peace treaty with the new German nation). "With pallid faces and trembling hands they wrote their names quickly and were then conducted back to their places," so noted one of the American delegates. Wilson was next to step forward to sign the peace treaty – now officially known as the Treaty of Versailles – followed by the other delegates with the exception of the Chinese delegation who had refused to sign because they were unhappy with the arrangements with Japan over the Shantung Peninsula.

The signing of the Treaty of Versailles brought to a close the first and most important stage of the peace process but the conference continued without the presence of the senior statesmen until January 1920. There were still treaties with Austria, Hungary, Bulgaria and Ottoman Turkey to finalize.

Down to Business

The Treaty of Versailles created nine new nations – Finland, Hungary, Austria, Yugoslavia, Czechoslovakia, Poland and the Baltic nations of Estonia, Latvia and Lithuania. The Paris Peace Conference, however, left many loose ends especially in the centre of Europe where geopolitical tensions and civil unrest muddied the waters. The talks failed to establish the territorial boundaries of Ukraine, Georgia, Armenia and Belarus. All four countries were formerly vassals of the Russian Empire before they were ceded to Germany under the Treaty of Brest-Litovsk. The latter was nullified by the Treaty of Versailles leaving these four "buffer states" lying between Russia and Central Europe in a state of flux; their boundaries at the time were fluid, and the military and political situation in these "buffer states" was still evolving. Civil war had broken out in Ukraine and Russia. Ukraine (unlike Poland) was not specifically covered by Wilson's Fourteen Points and as pointed out by Professor Margaret MacMillan in her seminal book *Paris 1919,* Wilson's nemesis, Senator Henry Cabot Lodge, was in favour of an independent Ukraine which may have provoked Wilson to stand firm on his default position of "self-determination". In the event poor Ukraine, the largest country in Europe save for Russia, was left to wither on the vine. The Bolsheviks would ultimately gain the upper-hand in both Ukraine and Russia when in 1922 the former became a satellite state of Soviet Russia only gaining its independence with the dissolution of the Soviet Union in 1991.

The completion of the signing ceremony was announced to the waiting crowds by the firing of canons. After posing for official photographs with Lloyd George, Clemenceau and Orlando, the Wilsons drove back to their temporary residence in Paris. All along the route crowds cheered as their motor convoy passed. Wilson turned to his wife and said: "Well, little girl, it is finished, and, as no one is satisfied, it makes me hope we have a just peace; but it is all in the lap of the gods." Later that day the presidential party boarded the overnight train for the port of Brest as a military band played *The Star-Spangled Banner*.

Down to Business

On the morning of June 29, 1919, the Wilsons were welcomed on board the *George Washington* which was to take them back to New York. Woodrow Wilson would never again set foot on European soil. Six months spent away from the White House negotiating a treaty designed to bring order and peace to a troubled and war-torn Europe had taken a heavy toll on the president both physically and mentally.

Signing of the Treaty of Versailles in the Hall of Mirrors by John Christen Johansen (1876-1964) depicting the American delegation (Pershing, Bliss, Wilson, House, White and Lansing).
Credit: National Portrait Gallery Smithsonian Institution NPG 65 83

Chapter Eight

Taking on the Dissidents

As the *George Washington* steamed out into the Atlantic, Woodrow Wilson's thoughts turned towards those recalcitrant Republican senators whose hostility to the treaty and more especially the League of Nations threatened to undermine the hard work he and the other leading statesmen had undertaken in Paris. Since his brief return to the States in March, public opinion had moved decidedly in favour of ratification. Despite public support for the treaty the majority of senators – mainly Republican – opposed ratification.

Opposition to the treaty centred mainly on Article X which dealt with the League of Nations. Those opposing the treaty claimed that the independence of the United States would be fettered by Article X which required each participating nation to "respect and preserve as against external aggression the territorial integrity and existing political independence of all Members". The opponents of the treaty reasoned that Article X ceded Congress's power to declare war to the Council of the League of Nations. The senators who opposed the treaty fell into two sub-groups – those who wanted no truck with the League whatsoever regardless of any future changes to the wording of Article X, and those who would support ratification of the treaty subject to Article X being amended to accommodate their concerns. The first group were known as "the irreconcilables" and the second more moderate group "the reservationists".

On July 8, the *George Washington* arrived at her berth in New York. Tumultuous crowds lined the sidewalks to welcome home the presidential party. A blizzard of ticker-tape rained down on the presidential motorcade as it progressed through the streets of Manhatten to Carnegie Hall where Wilson made a brief speech. Later that day the president and his party boarded a train for Washington. At midnight the train carrying the presidential party arrived at Union Station where a crowd estimated to be one hundred thousand strong greeted the president's homecoming.

Taking on the Dissidents

The rapturous homecoming may have emboldened the president to redouble his efforts to persuade dissident Republican senators to ratify his cherished League of Nations. Wilson opened his campaign on July 10 by presenting the treaty to an open session of the Senate. In a thirty-seven minute address Wilson failed to change Republican minds. "Soap bubbles and a souffle of rhetorical phrases" one unkind Republican called it. By Wilsonian standards it was a lacklustre speech full of abstract phrases with little or no substance. One congressman thought that Wilson had given the wrong speech at the wrong time and in the wrong place.

As the summer of 1919 wore on, Wilson was confronted with a myriad of domestic issues that took precedence over his campaign to obtain Congressional ratification of the peace treaty. In the northern industrial cities race riots were endemic. The National Guard was called out to support the army in quelling the violence that was engulfing African American neighbourhoods. Inflation was eroding living standards, a railroad strike was on the cards and unemployment was rising rapidly. All this was feeding into a general dissatisfaction with Wilson's presidency. On August 8, Wilson addressed a joint session of Congress but his peroration supporting ratification was poorly received, not helped by a rambling delivery that failed to articulate a coherent message. It was the last speech Wilson would deliver to Congress in person. His health broken, Wilson decided not to seek reelection at the end of his second term.

Suffering from nervous exhaustion, Wilson continued to press Republican senators to change their minds and support ratification. The opposition was led by the influential Republican senator, Henry Cabot Lodge, who felt that the United States by entering into the peace treaty was ceding sovereignty to the League of Nations. By now Wilson had given up on the irreconcilables but he reasoned that the moderate reservationists were more open to persuasion. The president went on a charm offensive but the reservationists stood their ground. They would only support "qualified" ratification. Wilson was not prepared to countenance changes to the text of the treaty, nor entertain qualifications attached to ratification. He was reluctant to go back to the main signatories to reopen negotiations on the League of Nations. Such a move, even if Britain, France, Italy and Japan were in agreement, would inevitably delay ratification. The moderate reservationists and Wilson had reached an impasse. Ruling out compromise – which many historians have since regarded as a gross act of folly – Wilson decided to take his case to the people over the heads of senators.

On August 27, the White House announced that the president would undertake a national speaking tour starting in early September. Edith and Dr Grayson had series misgivings about the planned tour fearing for the president's health. One experienced travel journalist noted how unwell Wilson seemed and (presciently) warned that "you are too ill to take that long trip. The heat will be intense in Ohio, Indiana, Illinois, Iowa and Nebraska. You will break down before you reach the Rockies." Edith and Grayson tried to talk the president out of the tour but he dug in his heels. He was adamant that not to tour the country would be an act of betrayal to the brave soldiers who took up "arms to end a war to end wars..... and he [would] never be able to look those boys in the eye".

The presidential train steamed out of Union Station on the night of September 3. The president was accompanied by his wife, Dr Grayson, a compliment of White House staff including servants, cooks, stenographers and secret service agents and Wilson's aide-de-camp, Joseph Tumulty, a larger than life Irish Catholic who also served as press secretary. It was planned that Wilson would make at least one major speech each day of the one month-long tour.

For a man in poor health and prone to strokes such a gruelling tour was courting disaster. Grayson was so concerned about his patient's health that he vetoed impromptu addresses from the rear platform of the train.

Taking on the Dissidents

As the presidential train made the long haul between Minneapolis-St. Paul and the Pacific Northwest, Wilson's health worsened; he was now suffering cardiac failure, having trouble breathing and constantly nursing splitting headaches. On reaching Seattle, Dr Grayson recorded in his diary: "....his exertions were sapping his vitality very fast". A trade union representative who met Wilson observed, "The president's head seemed heavy on his neck.....and he looked old – just old. Furthermore, one of his hands shook so badly that he had to grip the lapel of his coat to steady it, and for a few moments he closed his eyes as though he had a terrible headache."

Any sensible president would have called off the speaking tour at this juncture but not this president who with evangelical zeal ploughed on with his campaign to educate the electorate on why ratification of the Treaty of Versailles was an essential prerequisite to preventing another major war. At San Diego, Wilson addressed a crowd of thirty thousand who had gathered in an outdoor stadium. For the first time Wilson used a microphone attached to electric amplifiers to deliver his indefatigable message.

On reaching Los Angeles, the Wilsons exchanged the presidential train for a two-night stay in a local hotel. In July 1915, Wilson's close confidant and friend up until his second marriage, Mary Hulbert (the former Mrs Peck), had gone to live in California to be close to her only son; she was living alone in Hollywood in reduced circumstances, and her once magnetic personality that had men flocking to her dinner table had lost its allure. The Wilsons invited Mary to join them and Dr Grayson for lunch. "She came – a faded sweet-looking woman who was absorbed in an only son," Edith later recalled in her book of memoirs. Mary Hulbert for her part was more complimentary. "Mrs Wilson was not in the least as I expected to find her....she was much more junoesque, but handsome, with a charming smile that revealed her strong, white teeth. She was without question, a woman of strong character". During the lunch, Mary recounted her troubles to which Wilson exclaimed, "God, to think that you have suffered because of me." Following lunch, Edith accompanied her once rival to the elevator which Mary Hulbert later recalled in her autobiography "......quickly dropped me out of the life of my friend Woodrow Wilson - for ever".

Later that evening, Wilson complained to Edith that his headache was "unbearable". The doctor was called who found his patient "in a highly nervous condition, the muscles of his face were twitching, and he was completely nauseated". Edith later recorded: "That night was the longest and most heart-breaking of my life." Grayson informed Joe Tumulty that the president was is no condition to continue the tour. A tearful Wilson agreed. Tumulty issued a statement to the press corp to the effect that the rest of the tour was being cancelled because the president's exertions had brought on "a nervous reaction in his digestive organs". Tumulty's statement to the press was disingenuous. Dr Grayson must have known, or should have known even though he was not trained in neurology, that the statement was misleading. The train driver was instructed to return to Washington DC post-haste.

The president on returning to the White House after his aborted speaking tour was too poorly to fulfil his presidential duties. Dr Grayson prescribed rest. Edith was at her wits end. "My husband wandered like a ghost between the study at one end of the hall and my room at the other. The awful pain in his head that drove him relentlessly back and forth was too acute to permit work, or even reading," she later recalled.

On October 2, the president fell and lost consciousness. He had suffered a near-fatal stroke. The warning signs had been there ever since the Peace Conference in Paris, or even going back to the stressful period when as president of Princeton University he fought tooth and nail to get the university to adopt his reform program. A neurologist was summoned to the White House who confirmed after a second examination that the president had indeed suffered a stroke in the right side of his brain leaving the president's left side of his body paralysed, his vision and speech impaired and his mental state confused.

Chapter Nine

Cover-Up

Article II, Section I, Clause 6 of the United States Constitution states: "In Case of the Removal of the President from Office, or of his Death Resignation or inability to discharge the Powers and Duties of the said Office, the same shall devolve on the Vice President." Following the assassination of President John F. Kennedy, Article II was amended in 1967 to provide a more specific means of transfer of power when a president dies or is disabled. But back in 1919, there was sufficient ambiguity in the wording of Article II to permit the vice president to refuse to assume the office of presidency unless Congress passed a resolution that the office was in fact vacant and only after his personal physician certified in writing that the president was unable to discharge his powers and duties. Dr Grayson refused to sign a certificate of disability, and consequently no resolution was passed by Congress. Dr Grayson had by now become an intimate friend of the Wilsons. His refusal to sign a certificate of disability may have owed more to his friendship and loyalty to the Wilson family than his professional responsibilities. Edith Wilson – whose formal education was rudimentary and had taken no interest in politics – had on marrying her second husband placed his health, happiness and well-being above all other considerations including affairs of state, party and country. Edith's love for her husband was unconditional and perhaps she sensed that had her husband, a proud man with a stubborn temperament, been involuntarily removed from office on the grounds of disability that act alone more than the stroke itself would have hastened his early death. Edith and Dr Grayson acting as co-conspirators hid from members of Wilson's cabinet, members of Congress, the press and the American public the true extent of the president's illness and disability.

From October 1919 to the end of Wilson's second term on March 4, 1921, Edith managed the office of the president. Later she described her role as one of "stewardship". She acted as the president's gatekeeper, vetting communications and state papers and only putting before her husband material she deemed important enough to bring to his attention. In her role as gatekeeper, Edith only permitted a narrow circle of loyal associates access to her husband's bedside. Even Joe Tumulty was not permitted to see the president until mid-November. Subsequent historians and scholars have formed a view that Edith understated her role in her husband's presidency. It is true that she did not make critical decisions but she had enormous influence when it came to domestic and foreign policy by virtue of being the president's gatekeeper and steward. Nowadays it is highly unlikely that such an extraordinary state of affairs where the president's spouse assumes the role of *de facto* president where the *de jure* occupant of the White House is prevented through illness from fulfilling the duties of the office of president.

By December, Wilson was able to take his first tentative steps since the stroke. Christmas was not celebrated. Whilst the president's physical condition showed signs of improvement, his mental state was still confused. Following Wilson's illness in Paris when he was confined to his bedroom he began to display signs of paranoia. Waiters, porters, cleaning ladies and women who served him and Edith were in his mind secret agents spying on him. Now confined to his sickbed in the White House, Wilson held similar preposterous thoughts.

Throughout the early part of 1920, Edith kept the presidential show on the road with the connivance of Dr Grayson and Joe Tumulty. She engineered the removal of the secretary of state after he conducted a series of cabinet meetings without the president being in the chair. She refused to allow the newly appointed British ambassador, Sir Edward Grey (Britain's former foreign secretary), to present his credentials to the president in accordance with diplomatic protocol. Apparently Edith had taken exception to Grey because one of his military aide's at the Paris Peace Conference told a joke about her which was in bad taste.

In February a urologist from John Hopkin's finally let the cat out of the bag. He informed a reporter that the president had suffered a "cerebral thrombosis". This disclosure set-off a chain reaction which called into question the president's ability to carry out his duties. Meanwhile, domestic problems were piling up in the president's in-tray. Inflation was eroding living standards, strikes and unemployment were playing

This photograph was taken eight months after Wilson's near-fatal stroke. The depiction is misleading in that it was released to reassure a sceptical Congress and the public that it was business as usual at the White House. In fact it was shameful propaganda – the president was still seriously incapacitated both physically and mentally, and incapable of discharging his presidential duties.

havoc to the domestic economy and all the while the occupant of the White House was in la-la land.

On March 19, 1919, the Senate after a six hour debate and for the third and final time rejected the Treaty of Versailles. Forty-nine senators voted in favour of ratification and thirty-five against – seven votes short of the two-third majority required for ratification. It was the first time the Senate had repudiated a peace treaty. The failure to ratify meant that the United States was still technically at war with Germany and would have to enter into a separate peace treaty to bring a formal end to the war. On hearing the news, Wilson called Dr Grayson to his bedside, "Doctor, the devil is a very busy man."

By April, Wilson was feeling strong enough to hold his first cabinet meeting since his stroke. He sat at his desk in his study and did not stand up when cabinet members filed passed. His contribution to the discussions was modest and one cabinet member thought "He looked like a very old man and acted like one." Another member reflected, "It was enough to make one weep to look at him."

As spring turned into summer, Wilson grew physically stronger; he was now walking with the aid of a cane although his left arm was still paralysed. His cognitive functions, however, showed no signs of improvement. At times his sudden outburst of temper bordered on insanity. Having previously dismissed the idea of running for a third term he was now mulling-over in his own mind the prospect of entering the 1920 presidential race. He even went as far as writing down in shorthand the case for seeking another four years as president. This from a man who was mentally incapable of writing a speech let alone delivering it on the campaign trail. That the president could seriously contemplate a third term was axiomatic of a deluded mind. When news reached Grayson and Tumulty that the president was contemplating a third term they sprung into action to head off at the pass this hair-brained scheme before the charge gathered momentum. Grayson, who postulated that the campaign "would probably kill him" contacted an influential democrat and friend for help in persuading Wilson not to run.

The 1920 Democratic Convention was held in San Francisco. Right up to its opening in June, Wilson held out the prospect of being nominated. But as the convention got underway Wilson's devoted democratic friends felt that any move to nominate him would be a mistake and would "mar his place in history". Wilson was upset that his name had not been included on the ballot and blamed cabinet members for killing his dream. As it turned out Democratic Governor James Cox of Ohio won the party's nomination on the forty-fifth ballot. Franklin D. Roosevelt, the rising star of the party and who would go on to win four consecutive presidential elections, was nominated for vice president.

The 1920 election (the first where women had the right to vote in all forty-eight states) was between Cox and the Republican Senator Warren Harding. The latter won by a landslide with sixty per cent of the popular vote. Wilson did his best to turn the election into a referendum on membership of the League of Nations but by now the American public had other fish to fry. They were losing interest in foreign policy as domestic post-war troubles came to dominate the news agenda. The economy was in deep recession and across the nation there was considerable discontent with the government headed by a lame-duck president.

Woodrow Wilson still had another four months of his term to serve. With the republicans now controlling Congress, the president more than ever found himself marginalised. He soldiered on as best he could. Ray Standard Baker was shocked when he saw Wilson at the end of November. "A broken, ruined old man, shuffling along, his left arm inert, the fingers drawn up like a claw, the left side of his face sagging frightfully. His voice is not human: it gurgles in his throat.....And yet his mind seems as alert as ever."

.

Cover-Up

Marginalised, politically impotent and now in the dying days of his administration, the president's thoughts turned to the time when he would no longer occupy the White House. The war and the demands of the presidency had prevented him from revisiting his "beloved Lake District". In September Wilson wrote to the proprietor of the Rothay Hotel, Grasmere informing him that he hoped to visit the Lake region in April next year and would it be "possible....to accommodate my little party at that time. The party will consist of Mrs Wilson and myself and Mrs Wilson's brother.....I retain the most delightful memories of my former stay with you, and have only to beg that you will regard the information contained in this letter as private, inasmuch as it is my desire to travel next year *incognito*."

The Wilsons were beginning to fret about their financial situation when Woodrow was no longer in receipt of his presidential salary. In those days Congress did not provide an outgoing president with a pension. In December, Wilson received an early Christmas gift of $40,000 courtesy of the Norwegian Nobel Committee who awarded him their peace prize "for his role as founder of the league of Nations." The recipient of the award was too poorly to travel to Oslo to accept the award in person. In his telegram of acceptance to the Nobel Committee delivered by the United States ambassador to Norway, Wilson said that he accepted the award with "profound gratitude" but he acknowledged the need for further work to "rid [mankind] of the unspeakable horror of war." The only other sitting president at the time to receive a Nobel peace laureate was Theodore Roosevelt.

As her husband's second term was drawing to a close, Edith with the help of her property specialist brother went in search of a new abode. The Wilsons had considered moving to New York – even Boston and one or two other cities – but in the end they decided to stay put in Washington as it was convenient for the Library of Congress where Woodrow could carry out research into a new book project he had in mind. Washington was also the home of Edith. Wilson had informed his wife that upon retiring from the presidency he intended to write a book on government which he would dedicate to her. Like so many of his post-retirement plans the book project never got off the ground. However, Edith and her brother were successful in finding a substantial three-storey, brick built town house at 2340 S Street, NW. The house was bought unseen by Wilson with the help of financial contributions from his political friends. Wilson gifted the house to his wife in December 1920.

The inauguration of president-elect Warren Harding was held on Friday, March 4, 1921. It was a bitterly cold day. The spectators lining Pennsylvania Avenue caught sight of the outgoing president as he rode beside the younger and fitter Harding in an open-top automobile from the White House to the Capitol. It was the first time Wilson had been seen in public since his nation-wide speaking tour. The spectators were aghast to see a man severely emaciated, a mere shadow of his former self. "A living ghost" is how one reporter described the outgoing president. Wilson did not attend the actual swearing in ceremony of the 29th president of the United States. The weakness in his left leg prevented him from climbing the stairs leading to the east portico of the Capitol.

Later that morning ex-president Wilson and the former first lady accompanied by Dr Grayson, Joe Tumulty and a valet arrived at their new residence on S Street where a crowd of admirers had gathered outside. To the sound of cheering the Wilsons entered the building which would serve as their new home for the next three years. The curtain had finally come down on Woodrow Wilson's ten years of public service.

Chapter Ten

Ebb-Tide

I have fought the good fight, I have finished the race, I have kept the faith."
Paul (2 Timothy 4:7)

Edith Wilson did everything humanly possible to ensure that her husband's transition from the White House to his (their) new residence on S Street was relatively stress-free. A retinue of household staff – two night nurses, two servants and a chauffeur – were engaged. Edith's bachelor younger brother, John Randolph Bolling, was retained to provide full secretarial support to her husband. Dr Grayson was on call should his services be required. President Harding had gracefully agreed that *Admiral Grayson, who was still on active naval duty, could continue his role as physician to the ex-president.

Wilson was cared for by a male servant whose wife was Edith's servant. Edith Wilson in her memoirs pays, in language redolent of her 19th-century southern upbringing, tribute to them. "Fate was kind. I had been able to get a couple I had long known and to whom I here pay a tribute of gratitude and affection. They are Isaac and Mary Scott, of the best of the old-time coloured Virginia stock. They are still with me and I count them high on my list of this world's blessings. Scott was my husband's personal servant, and Mary, his wife, was, and is mine. From the moment Scott came in on that first day to assist my husband to undress and lie down, to the last tender service when Mr Wilson was on his deathbed, there was perfect fulfilment of every intimate duty....this gentle and understanding little servant became more and more essential to Mr Wilson's comfort."

The Wilson household quickly fell into a daily routine. Breakfast was followed by newspapers. Edith's brother dealt with the mail leaving Wilson to reply in person to ex-servicemen and one or two other correspondents. Visitors were seen after lunch, and around mid-afternoon Edith and Woodrow would board the Pierce-Arrow automobile for a drive. Wilson would insist that the chauffeur follow

*Formerly Captain Grayson but following promotion now Admiral Grayson.

134

the same route each day. The ex-president had predictability when it came to repeating over and over again the things he enjoyed doing. On one occasion when Woodrow was exploring England on his bicycle, Ellen urged her husband to visit the continent. "Why do you always go to the English Lake country: why not go to France, Italy etc.?" Her husband replied: "Are you never going to understand me and how I do not need to do a variety of things, but how I love most to do the thing I love best again and again."

The evenings were wiled away either watching movies in the library or Edith reading to her husband. Both Edith and Woodrow enjoyed vaudeville shows and many a Saturday evening would be spent at the theatre. Wilson's three daughters together with his cousin, Helen Bones, and his first wife's brother, Stockton Axson, were frequent visitors.

Before leaving the White House, Wilson decided to supplement his post-retirement income by setting up a legal practice in Washington in partnership with his former secretary of state, Bainbridge Colby. From the start Edith and Dr Grayson had serious reservations about the project which they felt would place on Wilson unnecessary stress. In show up Wilson invariably had ethical objections to taking them on. Such was Wilson's underwhelming interest in the law practice he only made one visit to the Washington office. Wilson's dalliance with practising law in Atlanta forty-years earlier was repeating itself. The reason his legal career came to a premature end then and why it was doomed to fail now was that Wilson had no appetite for vocational law. The two partners amicably agreed to dissolve the partnership.

In December, Wilson's old foe from his time in Paris paid him a visit. Georges Clemenceau, now aged eighty-one and retired from office, was on a speaking tour of the United States. He had not set foot in the United States in fifty-three years. "He looked younger than in 1919 and less grim and bitter," Edith later recalled. By all accounts Wilson was pleased to see the old "Tiger of France". However, Clemenceau was so taken aback by Wilson's appearance that he left after fifteen minutes and cancelled his evening engagements.

Despite his deteriorating health, Wilson still retained an interest in politics and followed closely the political contours of the new administration; he was never slow when the opportunity presented itself to lambast those politicians who repudiated the Paris peace treaty. The ex-president still nurtured the idea that one day he would return to frontline politics. Wilson had set his sights on running for president in 1924. When the penny finally dropped that Wilson was serious in pursuing a third term, Ray Stannard Baker wrote in his diary: "The sheer spirit of the man! Here he is, paralysed, blind in one eye, an invalid, 66 years old and sees himself leading a campaign in 1924!"

If President Harding was relishing a second term in the White House fate had other ideas. The spectators outside the Capitol on inauguration day could not fail to have noticed the difference in appearance between the ghost-like figure of the outgoing president and the president-elect who fair leapt up the Capitol steps while the older man resorted to a wheel chair to access the building. On August 2, 1923, the nation was stunned to learn of the sudden death of President Harding who was on an official tour of the West Coast. The 29th president of the United States died according to his doctor from a stroke although no autopsy was carried out at the request of his wife. A few days later Mr and Mrs Wilson in the company of Dr Grayson where driven to the White House where they joined the funeral cortege escorting Harding's body to the Capitol for the funeral service. Vice President Calvin Coolidge acceded to the presidency.

The following year David Lloyd George (no longer prime minister), his wife and their daughter, Megan, paid a visit to the Wilson household. They were instructed to keep their visit short. The former British prime minister was also shocked by Wilson's appearance. "Physically he was a wreck....." The two former leaders had a cordial conversation during which the ex-president railed about President Calvin Coolidge being a non-entity, and the deviousness of certain officials in the French delegation at the Paris Peace Conference. Lloyd George thought the outburst was insightful of "the old Wilson with his personal hatreds unquenched.... this extraordinary mixture of real greatness thwarted by much littleness".

Another British visitor to S Street was a rather nervous Prince of Wales, the future King Edward VIII and the late Queen Elizabeth II uncle. He was warmly received and put at ease by being shown Wilson's bed which had been made for Abraham Lincoln but in which the young prince's grandfather, Edward VII, had slept in.

Radio was still in its infancy when a nervous Woodrow Wilson gave his first ever radio address to the nation on the eve of Armistice Day 1923. It was the first time that the nation had heard the voice of its former war president. Wilson had been in bed all day with a pounding headache and was still in his dressing gown when he stepped up to the microphone placed by the broadcasters in his study. The speech lasted four minutes. He began his address by alluding to the happy memories of that November day in 1918 when the guns fell silent – the day when the horrific slaughter of the world war had at last come to an end. He then went on to deplore the United States for not joining the League of Nations but he hoped that America would come to its senses over time and eventually shoulder the burdens of global leadership – all too familiar themes he had been railing on about since Congress had rejected the peace treaty.

With his life ebbing away, Wilson turned to his former press secretary and renowned journalist Ray Stannard Baker about allowing him exclusive access his papers to enable him to write a posthumous biography. "I am glad to promise you that with regard to my personal correspondence and similar papers, I shall regard you as my preferred creditor, and shall expect to afford you the first – and if necessary exclusive – access to those papers.....I would rather have your

This photograph was taken in 1923 and shows Wilson riding in a Rolls-Royce which had been gifted by friends

The Wilsons participating in Armistice Day festivities

interpretation of them than that of anybody else I know, and I trust that you will not think it unreasonable that I should ask you to accept these promises in lieu of others which would be more satisfactory, but which, for the present, would be without practical value." Baker approached Edith about the project for unless the proposed biography had her blessing (which it did) he would not take on the onerous task.

By now it was evident to Edith that her husband's life was rapidly slipping away. So concerned that his death was imminent, she asked her brother to contact Wilson's children. Margaret and Eleanor set off for Washington immediately. Jessie and her family were in Asia and were notified by cable.

On Saturday, February 2, Wilson lapsed into semi-consciousness occasionally stirring to utter fragmented phrases. The last word to pass from his lips was "Edith". As the sun rose on Sunday morning and with the church bells ringing out across the nation's capital, Wilson lapsed into unconsciousness. He died at eleven fifteen. He was in his sixty-eighth year. Present at his bedside were Dr Cary Grayson and two nurses, his daughter Margaret (Eleanor arrived after her father's death) and Edith. Fifteen minutes after his death his dear friend Dr Grayson stepped out of the house and in floods of tears and in a trembling voice announced to the reporters and well-wishers who had gathered on the street that the end had been peaceful. He gave the underlying cause of death as arteriosclerosis.

President Coolidge offered to arrange for Wilson's body to lie in state at the rotunda of the Capitol and for burial at Arlington. Edith declined the offer for she wanted a brief private service at her home on S Street. At three o'clock on Wednesday afternoon, February 6, members of the family and long-standing friends, President Coolidge and the first lady, officials and former members of Wilson's cabinet gathered in the house on S Street. Colonel Edward House was not invited, nor at first was Wilson's former chief-of-staff, Joseph Tumulty, whom Edith had fallen out with but under pressure from her late husband's son-in-law, William Gibbs McAdoo, relented. Wilson's nemesis, Senator Henry

Cabot Lodge (who had been nominated to represent the Senate) was not invited by Edith who in a curt note wrote: "Realizing that your presence would be embarrassing to you and unwelcome to me, I request that you do not attend." Two ministers of the Presbyterian Church conducted the service. After the service the cortege set off for the Washington National Cathedral (which in 1924 was still under construction.) Following a brief Episcopal Ritual for the Burial of the Dead, Wilson's coffin was placed in the crypt of the cathedral. Dr Cary Grayson was the last mourner to leave the site of the interment. Hours before his death, Wilson turned to his doctor and friend, "You have been good to me. You have done everything you could." Wilson's coffin would remain in the crypt until 1956 when it was removed to its final resting place below a stone sarcophagus placed in the nave of the cathedral.

The sarcophagus of Woodrow Wilson in the south nave of Washington National Cathedral

Epilogue

Edith Bolling Wilson outlived her husband by thirty-seven years. She continued to live at S Street until her own death. In the summer of 1925, Edith made her own "pilgrimage" to see for herself the beauties of Lakeland and the places her late husband loved so deeply. By being in "this wonderland of sweets hills" Edith was fulfilling vicariously her husband's yearning to show her this beautiful corner of England to which he was so devoted.

Bowness-on-Windermere where Mrs Woodrow Wilson stayed on visiting the Lake District in the summer of 1925

Edith committed her long widowhood to perpetuating her husband's legacy and defending his reputation from perceived attacks upon his character by his critics. At the beginning of their relationship, Edith gave a written pledge to her husband to stand by him "...not for duty, not for pity, not for honour – but for love – trusting, protecting, comprehending love". In marriage she was true to her word and in widowhood she stood by him to the very end.

As custodian of her husband's papers, Edith worked closely with his official biographer, Ray Stannard Baker. In 1938, Edith published with

Epilogue

the help of Baker her own memoirs. It took her ten years to write her memoirs which abruptly end on her husband's death. The book was not uncritically received. Some of the events described in her memoirs had been skewed by the author to fit her own narrative of glossing over some of her husband's shortcomings and canonising his achievements. One reviewer considered the book not "a document of historical importance" but "delightful" as a "collection of episodes".

Edith lived through the horrors of the Second World War which her husband prophetically foresaw. "I can predict with absolute certainty that within another generation there will be another world war if the nations of the world do not concert the method by which to prevent it."

Edith Bolling Galt engagement photograph 1915

She was present at Franklin D. Roosevelt's funeral held at the White House in April 1945, and was invited by president-elect John F Kennedy to his inauguration.

Edith Bolling Wilson died of heart failure on December 28, 1961 on what would have been her late husband's one hundred and fifth birthday. She was laid to rest next to her husband at the Washington National Cathedral. Edith bequeathed her S Street home to the National Trust for the Historic Preservation on the proviso that the property be converted into a museum honouring her late husband. She donated all her husband's papers and personal library of eight thousand books to the Library of Congress.

Epilogue

The year 2024 will mark the centenary of Woodrow Wilson's death. His impact on the world will once again be placed under the spotlight by historians, writers, editors, columnists and others. Wilson's presidency coincided with the greatest catastrophic event to descend on Europe since the Black Death. It is mainly through the prism of war that Wilson's achievements and triumphs, his failures and shortcomings are evaluated. Had Wilson served his two terms as president at a time of peace his place in history would have rested on his legislative achievements which at the end of his first term were not inconsiderable. He would have gone down in history as a reforming president but perhaps not a remarkable one.

The Great War elevated Wilson to a world statesman and placed him firmly in the pantheon of outstanding 20th-century American presidents. Wilson's call to Congress in the spring of 1917 to declare war against Germany ultimately changed the course of the Great War. Had the United States remained on the sidelines of the European conflict it is unlikely that the Anglo-French forces had sufficient numbers of combat troops to defeat a numerically superior German army. Russia's capitulation in 1917 allowed the German military commanders to transfer tens of thousands of surplus soldiers to the Western Front. The German onslaught unleashed against the French and British forward positions in the spring and summer of 1918 almost succeeded in breaking the four-year stalemate. The French army was staring defeat in the face and the British forces were being driven back towards the English Channel but unlike the British Expeditionary Force in 1940 they went on the offensive supported by the Americans who fielded two million troops along the Western Front. Without the intervention of the United States, the Allies could well have lost the war. It took the combined alliance of the United States, Russia (until October 1917), Great Britain, Canada, Newfoundland, Australia, New Zealand, South Africa, India, France, Italy and Japan to over-power Germany whose land army retreated back across the Rhine exhausted and demoralised but never broken enabling it to fight another day, just as Woodrow Wilson predicted.

Epilogue

Even had Wilson succeeded in his quest to obtain Congressional ratification of the Paris Peace Treaty, it is doubtful whether American membership of the League of Nations would have arrested a revanchist Germany in the 1930s. Germany never accepted the peace settlement of Versailles. The British cabinet sought at the last minute to ameliorate the draconian terms imposed on Germany but even had Wilson acquiesced and watered-down the terms of settlement it is unlikely to have changed the eventual outcome. Would a less harsh treaty have prevented Germany's unrepentant military and industrial overlords from rearming? Possibly not. The German Empire of *Blood and Iron* created by Otto von Bismarck had shallow democratic roots as Katja Hoyer reminds her readers in her book *The Rise and Fall of the German Empire 1871-1918*. Armed conflict was baked into the constitution. "Not through speeches and majority decisions will the great questions of the day be decided....but by iron and blood" in the prescient words of the Iron Chancellor. Prussian militarism was allowed to trample all over a weak parliamentary system of government. The Weimar Republic of Social Democrats and Liberals established in 1918 started well enough but when tested *in extremis* by the Great Depression of 1929 it was unable to prevent the inexorable rise of Hitler.

It would take another world war to bring about the total destruction of the German war machine. And it would fall upon the 32nd president of the United States having under his command the most powerful military force ever assembled to liberate Western Europe from tyranny and set Germany on a true democratic course – a course that over eight decades has brought peace and prosperity to the nations of Western Europe. On hearing that Woodrow Wilson would surely have raised his hat and given the broadest of smiles.

Sources and Acknowledgements

My first debt is to my infinitely patient wife Heather who over the past eighteen months or so has been living with two men – a self-obsessed husband who has been struggling to complete his "Wilson Project" and a statesman who bestrode the world stage over a hundred years ago but, sadly, nowadays is barely remembered by the majority of people in Britain. Even the two greatest statesmen of the 20th-century, Winston Churchill and Franklin D Roosevelt, are fast receding into the mists of time. School children in Britain today are more likely to associate the name *Churchill* with a nodding dog used by an insurance company to promote its products than the prime minister who led Britain to victory during the Second World War.

I owe an immeasurable debt to the late Andrew Wilson whose book *A President's Love Affair with the Lake District* started my journey along the road leading to this publication. His book was a revelation.

In researching and preparing this book many articles, papers, books (printed and in electronic format), newspapers, journals, ordnance maps and websites were consulted. The following books I found extremely informative in researching my subject. After reading Andrew Wilson's book, I turned first to the American historian, Professor John Milton Cooper Jr., who is rightly regarded as the world's greatest authority on Woodrow Wilson. His biography on Wilson is in a class of its own. The book is beautifully written and the prose sublime. For those readers who wish to take a deep-dive into the life and political career of Woodrow Wilson then Professor Cooper's book is a must-read.

Hard on the heels of Cooper's biography, I read the highly acclaimed *The Moralist* by Patricia O' Toole. The sub-title of her book is *Woodrow Wilson and the World He Made*. It is a thoroughly engaging book, lucidly written with a strong focus on the First World War.

In writing about the Paris Peace Conference of 1919, I am indebted to the Canadian historian, Professor Margaret MacMillan, the great-granddaughter of David Lloyd George. Her book titled *Paris 1919: Six*

Sources and Acknowledgements

Months That Changed The World provides an engrossing account of the peace conference and the cast of characters who turned up. Rubbing shoulders with world leaders were the likes of Lawrence of Arabia and an unknown kitchen chef from Vietnam called Ho Chi Minh. MacMillan's book is a masterpiece, a tour de force and a must-read for those who wish to learn more about the peacemakers and their treaties which many historians consider to be the root cause of many of today's geopolitical tensions around the world.

I must also mention a book with the somewhat apocalyptic title, namely *Blood and Iron: The Rise and Fall of the German Empire 1871-1918* by the Anglo-German historian Katja Hoyer. In her brilliant book, Hoyer reminds her readers that the German Empire of "Blood and Iron" created by Otto von Bismarck had shallow democratic roots and that the system was "flawed from the outset, built on foundations of war, not fraternity". In writing the Epilogue to my book, I was very much informed by Miss Hoyer's concluding thesis that (in my words rather than hers) the parliamentary system of government in Germany was too weak to hold in check the flames of Prussian militarism fanned by the kaiser.

I owe a debt of gratitude to the staff manning the desk of the British Library's Reading Room at Boston Spa near Leeds for making available the books listed in the Bibliography under the heading "British Library" which I have consulted in executing this work especially *Brother Wilson* by Stockton Axson and edited by Arthur S Link published by Princeton University Press. This book is a mine of information on Wilson's Anglophilia and the tour of Great Britain in 1899 made by Stockton Axson and his brother-in-law.

Sources and Acknowledgements

I would like to thank the following organisations for granting permission to publish extracts from their publications.

The History Press, England for granting permission to republish excerpts from "The Rise and Fall of the German Empire 1871-1918" by Katja Hoyer.

Princeton University Press via the Marketplace platform for granting permission to republish excerpts from "Brother Wilson": A Memoir of Woodrow Wilson by Stockton Axson edited by Arthur S Link.

University of North Carolina Press via the Marketplace platform for granting permission to republish excerpts from "The Intimate Papers of Colonel House" Volume I Behind the Political Curtain 1912-1915 edited by C Hartley Grattan and Charles Seymour.

Every effort has been made to contact or trace all copyright holders. The author/publisher will be glad to make good any errors or omissions brought to their attention in future editions.

The Cottage
Follifoot   J.C.
Harrogate
North Yorkshire
HG3 1DQ
April 2023

Bibliography

British Library

Axson, Stockton. *Brother Woodrow: a Memoir of Woodrow Wilson* edited by Arthur S Link and published by Princeton University Press, William Street, Princeton, New Jersey (1993).

Wilson, Edith Bolling. *Memoirs of Mrs Woodrow Wilson* published by Putnam, London in 1939.

McAdoo, Eleanor Wilson. *The Priceless Gift: The Love Letters of Woodrow Wilson and Ellen Axson Wilson* edited by Eleanor Wilson McAdoo and published by McGraw Hill Book Company Inc. New York (1962).

House, Edward. *The Intimate Papers of Colonel House* arranged as a narrative by Charles Seymour Professor of History at Yale University, Volumes I, II and III published by Ernest Benn Limited, London.

Lloyd George, David. *Memoirs of David Lloyd George* Volumes I and II published by Oldhams Press Limited, London.

Grayson, Cary T. *Woodrow Wilson: an intimate memoir* by Rear Admiral Cary T Grayson (1977) published by Potomac Books, Washington.

Hulbert, Mary Allen. *The Story of Mrs Peck*: an autobiography (1933) published by Minton, Balch & Company, New York.

Library of Congress, Washington DC

Woodrow Wilson Papers (digitized)

Ray Stannard Baker Papers

Cary Travers Grayson Papers

Joseph Patrick Tumulty Papers

Edith Bolling Wilson Papers

White House Usher's Diary (1913-1921)

Bibliography

The White House Historical Association - Edward G. Lengal Chief Historian.

American Battle Monuments Commission. Remembering World War I: The U.S. Navy Arrives in Europe.

British Library Museum: The Challenge Accepted: President Wilson's address to Congress April 2nd, 1917.

Imperial War Museum - First World War.

Other Sources

Arnold, J O. The Merlewood Mystery published by Thomas Nelson and Sons Ltd. 1928.

Boissoneault, Lorraine. What Did President Wilson mean when he called for "Peace Without Victory" 100 years ago?" published in the Smithsonian Magazine under the heading World War I: 100 years later. January 23, 2017.

Cooper, John Milton, Jr. Woodrow Wilson a Biography published by Alfred A. Knopf, New York (2009).

Coppack, John. The Lake District of Adelaide Arnold published by Follifoot Publishing Limited 2020.

Coulter, Peter. BBC, Northern Ireland. Woodrow Wilson: a brief portrait of the 28th President of the United States 4 March 2013.

Fischer, John. The Golfing President: The Golf Heritage Society.

Hansard – UK Parliament.

Hoyer, Katja. Blood and Iron: The Rise and Fall of the German Empire 1871-1918 published by The History Press, Cheltenham, Gloucester (2021).

Kazin, Michael. War Against War: The American Fight for Peace, 1914-1918 published by Simon Schuster (2017).

Kennedy, Ross. "The Will to Believe: Woodrow Wilson. World War I, and the American Strategy for Peace and Security".

Bibliography

Lehrman, Robert. When Wilson asked for War by Robert Lehrman published in April 2017.

Link , Arthur S. Woodrow Wilson and the Progressive Era, 1910-1917.

Lynn, Kenneth S. The Hidden Agony of Woodrow Wilson. Essays/Winter 2004 Wilson Quarterly Archives.

MacMillan, Margaret. Paris 1919: Six months that changed the World published by Random House Trade Paperback, New York (2002).

Miller, Alisa. Kings College, London. International Encyclopedia of the First World War: Press Journalism (USA).

O'Toole, Patricia. The Moralist: Woodrow Wilson and the World He Made published by Simon & Schuster Paperbacks, New York (2019).

Parker, John. Cumbria: a Guide to the Lake District and its County published by Bartholomew 1977.

Perkins, Dexter (1939). The Peacemakers. The Virginia Quarterly Review.

Powell, Jim. CATO Institute: Policy Report: Woodrow Wilson's Great Mistake, May/June 2014.

Ransome, Arthur. Pigeon Post first published by Jonathan Cape London in 1936.

Rowse, A.L. The Story of Britain published by Tiger Books International 1993.

Saunders, Frances W. Love and Guilt: Woodrow Wilson and Mary Hulbert. Article dated April/May published in American Heritage, Volume 30, Issue 3.

Shachtman, Tom. Edith and Woodrow: A Presidential Romance. Putnam, 1981.

Trickey, Erick. Smithsonian Magazine Article headed "World War I: 100 years later". April 3, 2017.

Wainwright, A. Wainwright in the Valleys of Lakeland published by Michael Joseph Ltd 1992.

Wainwright, A. A Pictorial Guide to the Lakeland Fells Book Three "The Central Fells" published by the Westmorland Gazette.

Bibliography

Watson, Alexander, Goldsmiths, University of London. German Spring Offensive 1918: International Encyclopedia of the First World War 1914-1918, published May 2016.

Wilson, Andrew. A President's Love Affair with the Lake District in collaboration with S. Peter Dance published by the Lakeland Press Agency, Windermere, Cumbria (1996).

Wilson, Woodrow. "Correspondence Between the United States and Germany Regarding an Armistice (1918)." Source: The American Journal of International Law, Vol. 13. no 2. 1919, pp 85-96.

Wilson, Woodrow. British Library Museum: The Challenge Accepted: President Wilson's address to Congress April 2nd, 1917.

Wilson, Woodrow. New York Times: "American Neutrality" April 29, 1915 date of speech. Article appeared April, 21, 1915.

Wilson, Woodrow. Congressional Government: A study in American Politics published by Good Press. Originally published in 1885.

Wilson, Woodrow. Constitutional Government in the United States published by Read Books Ltd and Google Books.

Wordsworth, William. The collected Poems of Wordsworth. Google Books.

Websites:

Britannica Online
British Library
British History Online
Library of Congress
Smithsonian Magazine Online
Whitehousehistory.org
Wikipedia.org
Wikimedia.org
Wikimedia Commons

Photograph, Illustration and Image Credits and Sources

Page 5
Woodrow Wilson portrait 1919. Source Library of Congress.

Page 6
Pelter Bridge, Rydal, Cumbria. Author John Coppack (2020).

Page 16
White House South side. Author Matt Wade. File licensed under the Created Commons Attribution - Share Alike 3.0. Uploaded from Wikimedia Commons.

Page 19
Woodrow Wilson addressing a joint session of Congress on April, 2, 1917. Harris & Ewing Collection. Source Library of Congress.

Page 21
Sinking of the Lusitania. Engraving by Norman Wilkinson. The Illustrated London News May, 15 1915. Uploaded from Wikimedia Commons.

Page 35
Three British soldiers in World War One trench with grove of trees and hills in the background. Date 1918. Source Imperial War Museum.www.iwm.org.uk/collections/item/object/20079. Author Paul Nash (1889-1946). Open Library: OL846962A. Released to Wikimedia Commons.

Page 38
Watercolour by Belgian artist Alfred Theodore Joseph Bastien - "over the top". Credit Canadian War Museum. Uploaded from Wikimedia Commons.

Page 41
"Zonnebeke" painting by Sir William Orpen (1918) depicting the horrors of the Passchendaele campaign. Source Tate Britain. Public Domain. Uploaded from Wikimedia Commons.

Page 42
War Memorial, Beaune, France. Author John Coppack (2022).

Pages 46 and 51
President Woodrow Wilson. Source Library of Congress.

Page 54
Ellen Louise Axson. Source Library of Congress.

Photograph, Illustration and Image Credits and Sources

Page 56
Portrait of Jessie Woodrow Wilson Sayre. Photographer unknown. Date unknown.
Source Woodrow Wilson Presidential Library. Uploaded from Wikimedia Commons.

Page 61
Edith Bolling Galt driving her electric automobile. Source Library of Congress.

Page 63
Edith Bolling, full-length portrait LCCN93516290 jpg. Photographer Harris & Ewing.
Source Library of Congress.

Page 64
Edith Bolling between 1886 and 1896. Source Library of Congress.

Page 67
Dove Cottage, Grasmere, Cumbria. Author John Coppack (2022).

Page 70
Rydal Water, Cumbria. Author John Coppack (2022).

Page 71
Ullswater, Cumbria. Author John Coppack (2022).

Page 74
St Oswald's Church, Grasmere, Cumbria. Author John Coppack (2022).

Page 77
Furness Abbey. Author Vishnumukundan (October, 7 2007). Licensed without
conditions. Uploaded from Wikimedia Commons.

Page 79
Windermere from Loughrigg Fell. Author John Coppack (2022).

Page 81
Loughrigg Cottage, Rydal, Cumbria. Author John Coppack (2022).

Page 82
The River Rothay at Pelter Bridge, Rydal, Cumbria. Author John Coppack (2001)

Page 91 (top image)
The Wordsworth Hotel, Grasmere, Cumbria. Author John Coppack (2022).

Page 91 (lower image)
Townend, Troutbeck, Cumbria (National Trust). Author John Coppack (2022).

Photograph, Illustration and Image Credits and Sources

Page 86 (top image)
The upper reaches of the Troutbeck Valley looking towards High Street. Author John Coppack (2022).

Page 86 (lower image)
Troutbeck Valley. Author John Coppack (2022).

Page 87
Blue-bell lined path, Troutbeck, Cumbria. Author John Coppack (2022).

Page 92 (top image)
The Wordsworth Hotel, Grasmere, Cumbria. Author John Coppack (2022).

Page 92 (lower image)
Townend, Troutbeck, Cumbria (National Trust). Author John Coppack (2022).

Page 95 (top image)
Ennerdale Water and Scoat Fell by Peter S. Licensed under Creative Commons Attribution-Share Alike 2.0. Uploaded from Wikimedia Commons.

Page 95 (lower image)
Duddon Valley, Cumbria. Author Rosemary Duncan (September 20, 2008). Source: geograph.org.uk Licensed under Creative Commons Attribution Share-Alike 2.0. Uploaded from Wikimedia Commons.

Page 97
Governor Wilson, Ellen Wilson and their three daughters. Source Library of Congress.

Page 99
Paris procession. Source Harris & Ewing, Inc. Published between 1921 and 1924. Library of Congress Prints and Photographs Division.

Page 102 (top image)
President Wilson and King George V. (December 28, 1917). Photographer unknown. Source Cary T Grayson Collection. Library of Congress.

Page 102 (lower image)
President and Mrs Woodrow Wilson arriving in a horse-drawn carriage at the Mansion House, London. American official photographer (December 28, 1918). Library of Congress.

Page 105
South portal of Carlisle Cathedral. Author Martinvl (May, 31 2021). Licensed under Creative Commons Attribution Share-Alike 2.0. Uploaded from Wikimedia Commons.

Photograph, Illustration and Image Credits and Sources

Page 108
Paris Peace Conference of 1919. Council of Four: David Lloyd George, Vittorio Orlando, Georges Clemenceau and Woodrow Wilson. Author Edward N Jackson (US Army Signal Corps) May, 27 1919. Uploaded from Wikimedia Commons.

Page 113
Photograph of a painting by Sir William Orpen depicting Woodrow Wilson flanked by the prime ministers of France, Italy and Great Britain. The Council of Four members are positioned in front of the marble fireplace inside the Quai d'Orsay, Paris. Credit: Imperial War Museum, London. Uploaded from Wikimeda Commons.

Page 116
James Kerr-Lawson - The Cloth Hall, Ypres (CWM 19710261-0334) between 1917 and 1919. Credit Canadian War Museum. Uploaded from Wikimedia Commons.

Page 121
Signing of the Treaty of Versailles in the Hall of Mirrors by John Christen Johansen (1876-1964) depicting the American delegation. Credit: National Portrait Gallery Smithsonian Institution NPG 65 83.

Page 129
President Woodrow Wilson seated at desk with his wife June 1920. Source: Library of Congress.

Page 138 (top image)
Woodrow Wilson in automobile LCCN2016892966.jpg. Photographer Hams & Ewing (1923). Library of Congress.

Page 138 (lower image)
Woodrow and Edith Wilson participating in Armistice Day celebrations 1922. Source Library of Congress.

Page 140
Sarcophagus of Woodrow Wilson in the Wilson Bay of the South Nave of Washington National Cathedral. Author Tim Evanson (December 29, 2011). Source: https://www.flickr.com/photos/23165290@N00/6623015225/. Licensed under Creative Commons Attribution Share-Alike 2.0 generic license.

Photograph, Illustration and Image Credits and Sources

Page 141
Bowness-on-Windermere, Cumbria. Author John Coppack (2021).

Page 142
Portrait of Mrs Woodrow Wilson (1915). Source Library of Congress.

About the author

John Coppack was born in Lancashire and spent his early childhood in Liverpool. John holds an honours law degree from the University of London. He lives in Harrogate, North Yorkshire with his wife and daughter. Before taking up writing in his mid-fifties John held a senior position with an international healthcare group headquartered in the United States.

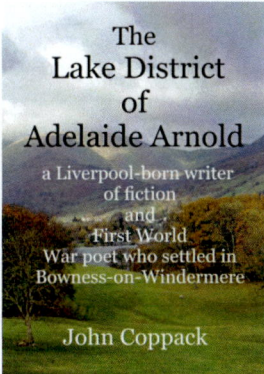

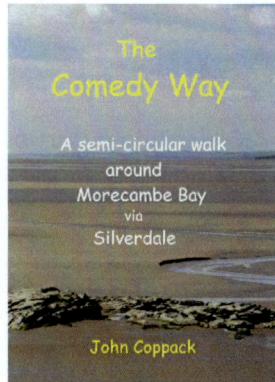

The
Lake District
of
Adelaide Arnold

a Liverpool-born writer
of fiction
and
First World
War poet who settled in
Bowness-on-Windermere

John Coppack

The
Comedy Way

A semi-circular walk
around
Morecambe Bay
via
Silverdale

John Coppack

Also by the author

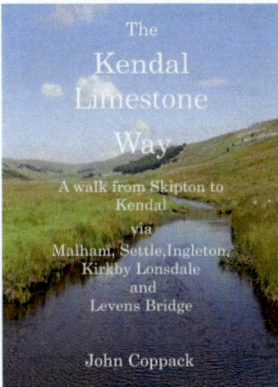

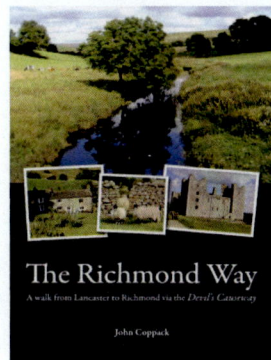

The
Kendal
Limestone
Way

A walk from Skipton to
Kendal
via
Malham, Settle, Ingleton,
Kirkby Lonsdale
and
Levens Bridge

John Coppack

The Richmond Way

A walk from Lancaster to Richmond via the *Devil's Causeway*

John Coppack